A HISTORY *of the* ENDURING WASHOE PEOPLE

AND THEIR NEIGHBORS INCLUDING
THE SI TE CAH (SASQUATCH)

GUY NIXON (REDCORN)

Library of Congress Control Number: 2013910469

ISBN:	Hardcover	978-1-4836-5146-0
	Softcover	978-1-4836-5145-3
	Ebook	978-1-4836-5147-7

This book was printed in the United States of America.

Rev. date: 07/17/2013

To order additional copies of this book, contact:
Xlibris LLC
1-888-795-4274
www.Xlibris.com
Orders@Xlibris.com
137015

Table of Contents

1. The Washoe Arrive at Lake Tahoe 4
2. Map of the primary Villages 12
3. The Washoe lifestyle and trade 14
4. Culture and Family Organization. 26
5. Plants and Crops of the Washoe 29
6. The Bow and Arrows used by the Washoe 33
7. Religion and the Shaman 40
8. Cave Rock 43
9. The Cave of the Giant (The Real Sasquatch) 44
10. The Coming of the other tribes 50
11. My Ancestors Involvement 53
12. Captain Sutter 59
13. The Flood of 1862 69
14. Tracking 82
15. The Singing Stones 86
16. About the Author 88
17. Bibliography 91

Pictured above the Author Guy Nixon (Redcorn) who has walked, worked and hunted the trails of the Washoe and Nissenan for 45 years and developed a great respect for these first people of the Sierra Nevada.

The Wa She Shu (People from here)

The Washoe People are possibly the oldest residents of California and Nevada.

Their ancestors probably arrived here more than 6000 years ago and finding a piece of heaven on earth at Lake Tahoe, they stayed. The Washoe language is part of the Hokan Language family; however, it is so different from the others that it is believed that they have been isolated from the others for an extremely long time. Archeology confirms that both the Martis Complex and Kings Beach Complex of Northern California and West Nevada are ancestors to the Washoe.

California Indian Library Collections

The Lake Tahoe that the Washoe people found was very different from the Lake Tahoe we see today. When the Ancestors of the Washoe arrived the Great Basin was a land of lakes and wetlands filled with North American Zebra, Camel, two species of bison; Mastodon and Mammoth.

California Smilodon (saber toothed cats) were common and remains have been found in several caves both in Nevada and California in the Washoe homeland.

The shore of Lake Tahoe (Da ow aga) had armadillos (Glyptodon) the size of Volkswagen Beatles grazing along it's beaches as well as giant sloth.

Pictured above a giant armadillo and to the right a fossil of one. To the left a mammoth the Washoe would have encountered. Below the Short Faced Bear.

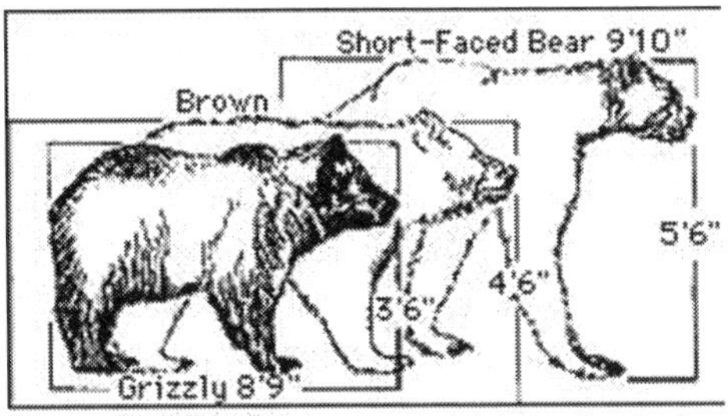

Figure 2:Relative size comparisons of grizzly, brown, and giant short-faced bears. Illustration by Ruth Ann Border, 1988.

Pictured above the short faced bear while to the left the common bison both of whom were living in the Carson Valley for several thousand years with the Washoe.

Pictured above are black Bears from the Washoe homeland. While not as aggressive as either the Short Faced bear or the Grizzly, black bears such as these can easily range from 400 to nearly 700 pounds and are very abundant today.
Below at left is a fossil and to the right an artists rendition of the long horn bison which roamed the Car-son Valley and meadows along Lake Tahoe when the Washoe arrived.

Pictured on this page are artists renditions and fossils of the great ground sloth. This species was very common along the shore of Lake Tahoe at the time of the Washoe's ancestors arrival.

Their ancestors had to avoid not only saber toothed cats and Grizzly bears but North American Lions, Cheetahs and the enormous Short Faced bear. The variety of megafauna found in the Tahoe Basin, California mountains, Sacramento Valley and Carson Valley was comparable to that of present day East Africa. Herds of bison would still be living in the Carson Valley as late as the 1820's, being the most Western extension of their range when Europeans arrived.

The giant ground sloth was very powerfully built and while a vegetarian was able to fight off the American Lions, Saber Toothed Cats and Short Faced Bears.

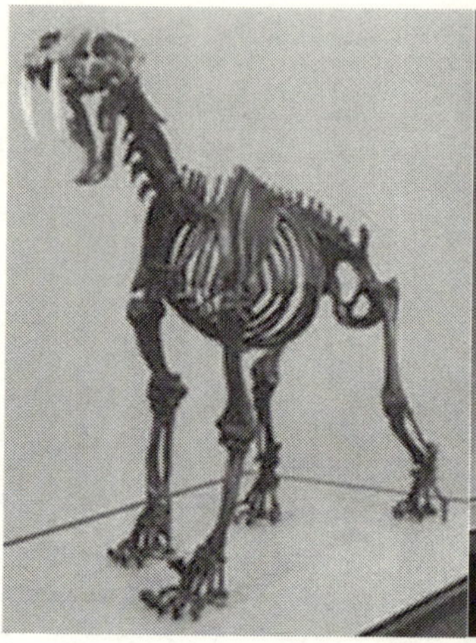

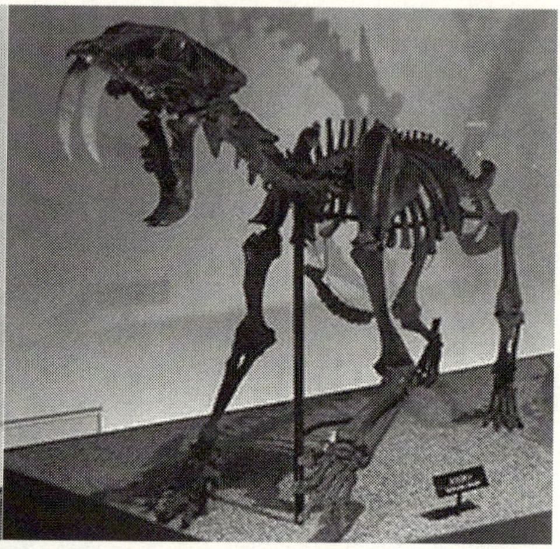

Pictured above the California Smilodon as fossils and an artists rendition.

For those interested there is a museum in the basement of the County Court House in Auburn, California, that has replicas of many of these fossils that children can hold and examine. These are replicas of fossils found in a cave along the North Fork of the American River.

Climate change is not a man made phenomena as most Modern Americans are led to believe. When the Washoe arrived the Farallon Islands were coastal foothills and California's coast line extended many miles further West. The forest they found was one of yellow pine but not the same species we see today.

After the Washoe's ancestors arrival the dry climate shifted to one of far greater precipitation. The Yellow pine species were crowded out by Red and White fir, Douglas Fir, Cedar, Sugar Pine and Redwood.

The Yellow Pine species their ancestors first saw went extinct in California, the only living offspring now exist in only two places, the Davis Mountains of West Texas and the the Sierra de la Laguna Mountains located just North of Cabo San Lucas on the extreme Southern tip of Baja California.

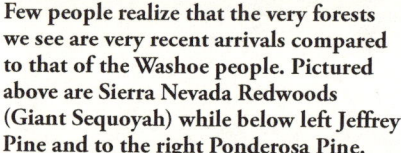

Few people realize that the very forests we see are very recent arrivals compared to that of the Washoe people. Pictured above are Sierra Nevada Redwoods (Giant Sequoyah) while below left Jeffrey Pine and to the right Ponderosa Pine.

The Washoe's land was now filled with forests of redwood and fir only to dry out again with new species of Yellow pine immigrating into their lands from the Sierra Madre Occidental of Northern Mexico. From these new immigrants would evolve the species we see today as Ponderosa, Jeffrey and Washoe Pine. I learned this and much more while working at the Institute of Forest Genetics in Camino California. To me it was amazing that the very species of Pine named for the Washoe Tribe is only a recent arrival compared to the Washoe people themselves.

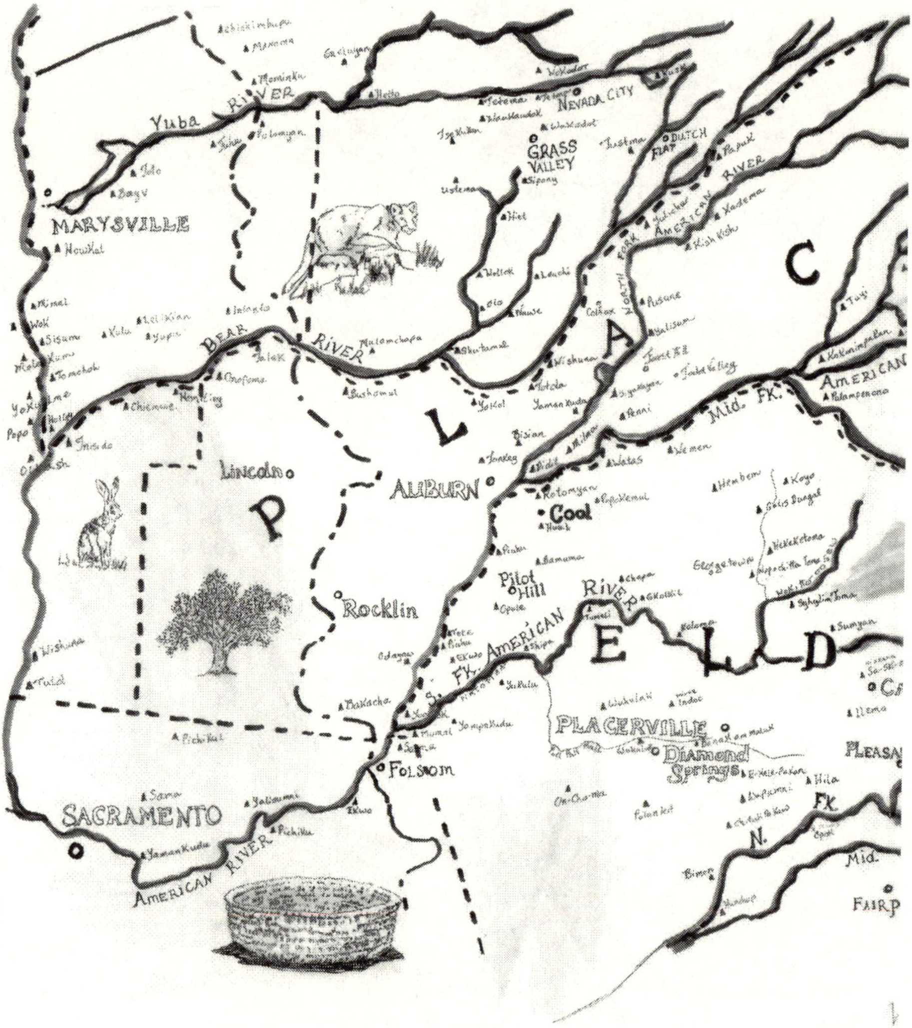

Yuba RIVER
MARYSVILLE
NEVADA CITY
GRASS VALLEY
DUTCH FLAT
NORTH FORK AMERICAN RIVER
BEAR RIVER
C
P
L
A
C
E
L
D
Lincoln
AUBURN
Cool
Pilot Hill
Rocklin
AMERICAN RIVER
S. FK.
Mid. FK.
AMERICAN
PLACERVILLE
Diamond Springs
FOLSOM
SACRAMENTO
AMERICAN RIVER
N. FK.
Mid.
Colfax
Georgetown

Village Sites of Hill Nisenan, Washoe and Miwok
El Dorado, Placer Counties

The Washoe Tribe

The Washoe Tribe was comprised of three bands.
The Welmelti (Northerners)
The Paw Lu (Those who spent their winters in the Carson Valley)
The Hungalelti (Southerners)

All three bands came together in the Lake Tahoe Basin for the spring (Am Suk),

Summer (Ci gah bet) and fall (O' osh) to take advantage of the re-sources available there. The three bands had distinctly different ac-cents from one another but mar-riages between the different bands was very common. It was the winter (Galais) that forced them to leave the Tahoe Basin to their winter villages. Appropriately called winter house (Galais Dun-gal), these were permanent settlements. Some people lived in the Galais Dungal year round while the majority of the population moved during the spring, summer and fall to harvest foods and conduct trading trips.

While the winter houses comprised fairly large groups, once they left for the seasons hunting and gathering they broke up into very small bands. These bands were headed by leaders who could be either male or female. Hunting was their business and Hunt Leaders had a leadership role that often extended beyond the scope of the actual management of the hunt. Both men and women hunted in Washoe society and men as well as women gathered Pinyon Pine nuts and acorns.

Even though the Washoe hunted deer, antelope, bighorn sheep, quail, grouse and sage hen, their primary game was rabbit. To the American of European descent this may seem strange but to those familiar with the Washoe home-land it makes complete sense. Jack Rabbits are extremely numerous in the lower elevations of the Washoe home-lands. To hunt the jack rabbits the Washoe employed several methods.

These all involved driving the jack rabbits either into nets, corrals or over cliffs.

Depending on the particular area it was and often is better to have a large number of drivers with several bands joined together to make Jack Rabbit drives. Every band had its own rabbit nets and by putting several bands' nets together a hunt was made far more efficiently. From my own experience hunting jackrabbits in this area one man might see only 15 to 30 rabbits stalking a section of creek bank while if done with three or four hunters, even later on the same day, the same stretch of creek bank produced more than 400 jackrabbits. The jackrabbit will circle around a lone hunter but with a number of hunters they will spook out and in numbers you would never believe other-wise.

The Washoe killed the rabbits with specially made clubs, similar to the Australian Aborigine's boomerang. The jackrabbit hides were then taken and cut into strips and woven untanned into blankets, shawls and other clothing.

(continued on p. 18)

Pictured above a boy with a big Jackrabbit. Below a length of rabbit net. Every band would have their own lengths of Rabbit netting and would join them together with those of other bands for communal rabbit drives.

Pictured above is Tankey Nisenan Huuk (Captain Tom) August 1874. The Jack Rabbit-fur robe may well be a trade item from the Washoe People. His headband is adorned with flicker and quail feathers. The medicine stick in back is covered with woodpecker scalps and flicker feathers. Around his neck is an abalone gorget.

The Jack Rabbit was a major source of food and clothing as well as a major trade item to tribes further West.

Pictured above Washoe getting ready for a Rabbit drive (Hunt).
Pictured below to the left two Washoe wearing Jack Rabbit fur blankets and to the right a Washoe with his bag of Jack Rabbits.

As the jackrabbit's hide strips shrank and twisted they made a cord with the long warm fur on the outside. Woven into a fabric the fur strips make a very warm comfortable blanket. As a point of fact Rabbit skin blankets were one of the Washoe's most lucrative trade items. Due in part to the low humidity rabbit skin blankets would last a rather long time in the Washoe homeland compared to the more moist Westside of the Sierra Nevada.

Jack rabbit meat has nearly no fat marbled in it and coupled with the low humidity it was easy to simply hang and dry the meat on wooden racks. Once dried the meat was pounded into meal that would be added to acorn or seed, flour to make soup or mush. Hundreds to thousands of jackrabbits make an incredible amount of protein.

In the 1930's the Dust Bowl destroyed thousands of family farms causing mass migration.

The majority of these people came West and by the time they arrived in this area they were often starving and in very poor condition.

Pictured above are Americans fleeing the environmental disaster of the Dust Bowl. As this population fled they became progressively more destitute and when they arrived here in the Washoe Homeland they were in poor physical condition. While the farmers and Ranchers here in the Washoe Homeland didn't have much they could conduct Jack Rabbit drives that generated enough to at least provide these people with protein.

Due to the economy these American refugees were forced to keep moving, as most of them ended up coming to California when they got to the Carson Valley they were in very poor shape and most didn't have the money to even buy the gas necessary to get over the Sierra Nevada.

These people had no money and no food. Many kind hearted local farmers and ranchers, some of whom were Washoe as well as my Grandfather, worked together conducting jack-rabbit drives to feed them. The rabbit meat was ground and mixed with any beef or pig fat that could be obtained to make burger, this was then used to feed these desperate people. Grandpa noted that in one rabbit drive they managed

Pictured below are jack Rabbits in a corral from a rabbit drive.
I have used this period of history to better illustrate what kind of a resource the Jack Rabbit can be and why it played such an important role in the Washoe peoples food supply.

to collect enough rabbit meat to feed nearly three hundred people for the better part of a week. This doesn't take into account the flour, vegetables and rice that was also donated but due to the poor economy and limited resources available to the local people it was the Jack Rabbit meat that made up the vast bulk of the food they provided.

Not that the local ranchers and farmers were eating much differently themselves. The generosity of these people should not be forgotten. Today it is difficult to realize just how important the Jack Rabbit has been as a food source. The jackrabbit's ability to reproduce like rabbits (technically they are hares) on limited forage, even in drought conditions, producing large quantities of protein has fed many families. In Oklahoma the Jack Rabbits were called Texas Buffalo as well as a few names I won't repeat here.

My first game animal was a Jack Rabbit which I carefully skinned, tanning the hide and eating the meat. My son's first game animals have also been jackrabbits. In this part of the world they are the most abundant game animal. This is why the jackrabbit was the primary game animal of the Washoe people.

Pictured above California Nelson Bighorn Sheep which lived around Lake Tahoe. Pictured below the Sage Hen which were numerous in the Eastern part of the Homeland.

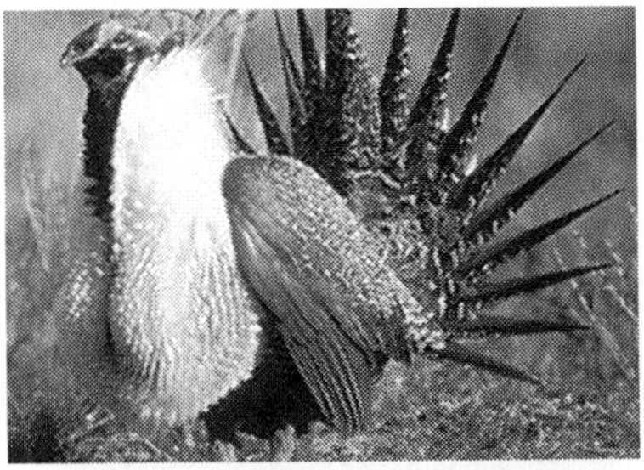

For the Washoe it was simply the effort to re-turn ratio that made the jackrabbit the primary game animal.

The Washoe also made drives for antelope, herding them into corrals. Deer were the primary big game animal and a Washoe boy was not considered old enough to be married until he was able to kill a mature buck. Deer skin was very desirable for clothing and moccasins as it was easier to work than the thinner antelope skin or the thicker bear skin.

In the mountains around Lake Tahoe and the Carson Valley there were California Bighorn Sheep and some Washoe were very adept hunters of these wild sheep.

The grizzly bear was a very dangerous animal and as such they were not particularly hunted but were killed in self defense and in the protection of the people's supplies of food

Pictured above a lion that was chasing school children to the right a Hill Nisenan quiver made from a lions tail.

Pronghorn were common in the Carson Valley

The black bear was hunted the but only men were allowed to eat the meat.

Mountain lion were hunted but not for neither their meat nor their skins in as much as they killed a number of Washoe women and children while gathering pine nuts and acorns. When gathering these crops the women were compromised as they could not see the approaching lion, while at the same time they did not look so much like people as deer, the lions primary food: Not that the mountain lions didn't eat they people they killed and by many tales and recent tragedies some lions even specialized in hunting people.

Sage hen were abundant on the East side of the Washoe homeland and ex-tensive effort was exerted in hunting them as well as trapping Mountain Quail and Blue Grouse. It was forbidden to kill a Golden Eagle as well as several species of owls.

In season the Washoe also gathered grasshoppers and locusts and considered the comb of several species of ground nesting hornets a delicacy. The hornet nest was typically subdued by setting it on fire, then once the adult hornets were eliminated the Washoe could remove the comb.

Pinyon Pine nuts (Tah Gum) and acorns were gathered in large quantities and could be stored for up to six years in sev-eral styles of granaries. As these crops were not consistent and one year may be fantastic while the next a complete loss, the storage of these crops in years of abundance was vita; however, these stores attracted bears and as such required guards year-round.

Several species of native bunch grass were cultivated by the Washoe and their seed collected to be ground into flour. The delta of the Walker River, where it empties into Walker Lake was extensively cultivated for several species of grass that produced edible seed. This cultivation had been done for thousands of years to the point that many of these species were in reality domesticated as once the Native people were removed these species declined to the point of extinction.

Pictured above the Tah Gum / Pinyon Pine Nut harvest 1902. The Tah Gum is still a very important part of Washoe culture.

Pictured above and below are examples of the Native Lahontan Cutthroat trout of Lake Tahoe, Truckee River, Pyramid lake.

Fishing was a major source of protein. It may surprise most people to know that the Kokanee Salmon they see in the stream profile at Lake Tahoe are not native to the area. These Salmon use Lake Tahoe as their ocean, make their spawn-ing run then die, Among the salmon are the native Cutthroat Trout who also spawn but do not die and instead return to the lake and river to continue living. These Native Cutthroat Trout grow huge and red colored, they have a wonderful pink meat that tastes much like ocean run steelhead, the Washoe also fished for Chub and Whitefish. Fishing the spawning runs was serious business and as it typically only lasts two weeks, the Washoe would even fish at night by the light of torches. This torch light was enough to enable the Washoe spearmen to see the flash of the fish. The spawning runs also brought in Grizzly Bears who were even more active a night making the torch light necessary to see the bears as well.

Trade

The Washoe made a good living as traders. Much like the Old Cherokee Nation the Washoe homeland is located in the mountains straddling the lowest passes that go through them. Both US 50 and I-80 as well as Highway 88 and several other passes go right through the Washoe Homeland. Straddling two very different regions the Washoe profited by the trade in goods between these regions. From the South near Mono Lake the Washoe had access to the volcanic cinder cones located just south of Mono Lake, one of the greatest sources of Obsidian in the world, ideal for making knives, arrow-heads and other tools. The Washoe got top value for bringing these quality obsidian blanks to trade at To Go No, present day Sly Park, California. Their other big trade item was jackrabbit skin blankets, these warm blankets were much sought after by the California tribes. The Washoe also traded pinyon pine nuts but these were more of a delicacy than a bulk food item.

The Washoe had great relations with the Hill Nisenan People who worked the only known quartz crystal quarry in the region, . These crystals were traded as far East as present day Denver Colorado, South to Baja California and North to the Rogue River. The Washoe had their finger on this trade item as it went East and they were known for this. The trade in quartz crystals, from this quarry, is believed to have been a major business for at least 800 years.

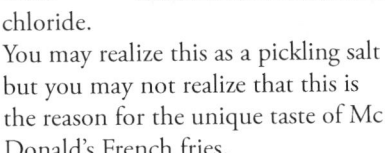

To the South in the Sierra Nevada were salt springs that the Mountain Miwok worked. By grinding holes into the rock ledges they channeled the salt water into these holes where it dried leaving the salt. This salt was highly prized as it was not the common sodium chloride such a sea salt but was primarily alum chloride. You may realize this as a pickling salt but you may not realize that this is the reason for the unique taste of Mc Donald's French fries.

For proof of this ask the establishment for a salt packet and read the ingredients, it is alum chloride not the more common sodium chloride. Yes, that special, nearly addicting taste

Pictured below a Mountain Miwok with salt harvest while pictured to the right some of the Miwok salt works located in the Sierra Nevada possibly worked for 3000 years. The extremely desirable salt being Alum Chloride.

is alum chloride and it isn't addicting just to humans. There are natural deposits of alum chloride in the Sierra Nevada such as the ones on Darling Ridge that draw deer in from miles to eat the earth, creating holes in the ground as they take in the alum chloride.

My Grandfather hunted deer over these natural licks on Darling Ridge and I have seen whole herds of deer working these licks. Four generations of our family have hunted this area!

The Mountain Miwok had a great product in this alum chloride and the trade in this special salt was a major industry. The Washoe's access to the source of this product was yet another commercial item of great value they had in their inventory.

Pictured above the author and his youngest son with buck taken near the Alum Licks located on Darling Ridge CA.

It is difficult for modern day man to realize the value of salt to these people. It wasn't used just for seasoning food, it was used for preserving food. We today salt our food to taste, in the past salt was used to preserve that food, salt was necessary in the preservation of skins, meat and fruits.

Crystals from the quarry located at Syhylim Toma have been found as far North as the Oregon Washington border and South to Baja California, trade with the coastal tribes extended information as well as goods.

The Coastal Tribes were able to produce sea food and products to trade for other goods from the interior tribes. The Washoe were situated in an ideal location to profit from this trade.

Pictured below is an example of a Washoe snow shoe and several arrow points. The larger ones are for hemoragic wounds while the smaller ones on the right are for using nuero toxin although they were also used without toxin for antelope hunting due the animals lighter build.

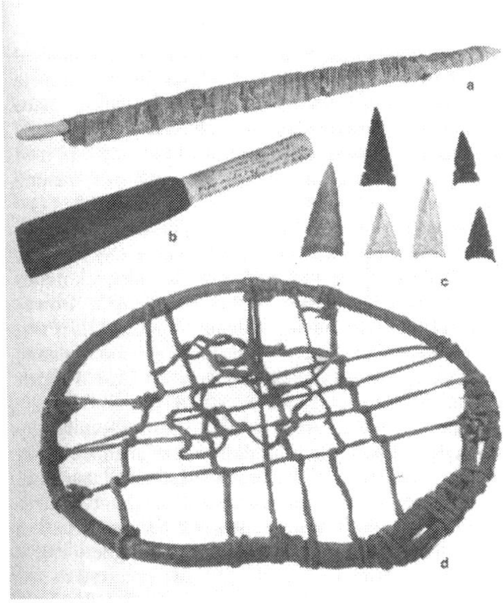

From the coast peoples the Washoe traded for smoked salmon and sea shells with abalone being the most prized sea shell. Whale and seal oil, acorn meal, elk hides, sea salt, and other items were in great demand by the peoples living in the Great Basin and Rocky Mountains to the East. The Washoe greatly improved their standard of living through this extensive trade network.

As a result of this incredible trade network the Washoe developed extremely effective snow shoes. These snow shoes enabled the Washoe to extend the time available for trading and hunting in the deep snow.

Fremont in his expedition across the Sierra Ne-vada had Washoe guides take him over today's Carson spur and Mormon Emigrant Trail to Sly Park, California. Fremont noted that he was greatly impressed by the Washoe's snow shoes and their agility on them.

Washoe Culture and Family Organization.

Typically a Washoe boy was not considered eligible to marry until he could kill a mature buck deer, showing his stature and ability to provide for a family. A Washoe girl was given a four day ceremony upon her first menstruation. When her second menstruation occurred her hair was cut and she was given an-other four day ceremony after which she was considered eligible to marry, most marriages among the Washoe were arranged. The different Washoe bands often came together for rabbit drives, fishing runs, gathering pinyon nuts or other crops and it was at these times that interested families would exchange gifts, if the gifts were accepted the young couple would start a courtship.

**Pictured to the left are Maidu.
The Washoe often intermarried with people of this tribe as both shared common resources and because the Washoe often used Maidu lands for their winter villages.**

After marriage the couple would usually live with the bride's family, this allowed the groom to demonstrate his ability to provide for her. Once the first child was born the couple might then move to live in another group or band, this was typical of marriages with people from other tribes. Coppa Hembo's father, a Hill Nisenan, married his mother, a Washoe, and after the marriage lived with her family in their village for some time until Coppa Hembo was born. Later the family moved to live in a Hill Nisenan Village, No Po Chitta Toma, some five miles to the South.

When a baby was to be born the mother would go to a small hut that had been built over a ditch in which a great deal of wood had been burned and the hot coals were covered with dirt.

This would provide a warm place for her to give birth.

The new baby was put into a cradle that was marked to indicate boy or girl. Typically the markings like (//////////////) were for a boy while (VVVVVVVV) were used for a girl.

The baby was usually not named until they could walk and the name was subject to change if they performed some great thing or event in their later years.

When a person died they were typical cremated, this was in part because burying the dead was nearly impossible due to the grizzly bears. As the body was burned it was poked with long poles to release the spirit while others wailed, this was called a Cry and was believed to scare away evil spirits who might try to capture the newly released spirit of their loved one. The Name of the dead person would not be spoken for many years because it was feared that their spirit would stay with the living and not realize it was dead. This custom of not speaking the name of the dead made keeping a history of these people very difficult.

The practice of cremation was very common in areas frequented by Grizzly Bears. The Idea of a Cry to keep evil spirits away from the newly released loved one's spirit was also a very common practice. Pictured below traditional religion continued these practices as seen in this picture from Colusa.

Plants and Crops of the Washoe

Camas bulbs

The Washoe were unique as they had access to many plants from different elevations on both the Eastern and Western side of the Sierra Nevada. The Washoe utilized more than 170 different plants.

Pigweed

In the lower elevations the Washoe cultivated and harvested camas bulbs, bitterroot, balsa and sego lily tubers.

The berries of the white and green leaf manzanita were gathered and ground into flour.

Sunflower

Wild Strawberries

The Washoe also gathered elderberries, chokeberries, gooseberries, golden currants, sierra plumbs and wild strawberries: all of which were eaten fresh but many could be made into dried preserves that would last for later consumption during the winter.

The so kop mi, a native potato, grows at higher elevations and was cultivated by the Washoe as a special food for new mothers.

Sierra Plums

Wild Onion was roasted and eaten while wild sun-flower, wild rye, and pigweed seeds were ground into flour to make unleavened bread.

In the spring wild mushrooms and rhubarb were eaten fresh. In the small streams and springs watercress grows and was eaten much of the year depending on the elevation.

The primary crops gathered by the Washoe were Pinyon Pine nuts and Acorns.

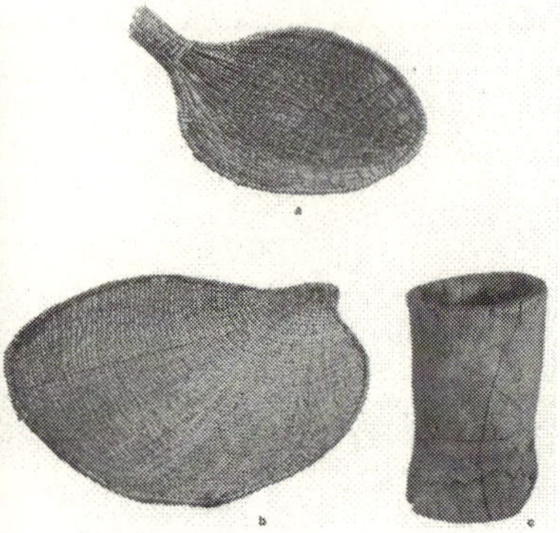

Pictured above Wuzzie George, a Northern Paiute, winnows Pinyon Pine nuts while below a Pyramid Lake Paiute woman removes native "wild" sunflower seeds by winnowing. To the right are some of the specialized beating, gathering and winnowing baskets designed for recovering and processing the seed of sunflower as well as two species of bunch grass. With the absence of cultivation at least four other species of grass have gone extinct that were domesticated in the Walker River Delta area where it drains into Walker Lake.

It is false to believe that the people of the Great Basin and Lake Tahoe country were primitive, they had in reality domesticated a number of native plant species and actively cultivated them.

Pictured to the lower right a Ute woman with an ergonomic basket

Pictured above Mabel Wright and Kathy Fraiser, both Pyramid Lake Paiute, gathering Pinyon Pine nuts. To the right Susie Dick, a member of the Washoe tribe from the Carson Valley, is seated behind a pine nut cashe.

Pictured to the right a woman thrashes rice grass then loads the grain into her burden basket.

Pictured below from left to right, the cracking open of the pine nut shells with a stone metatte, the shells are then winnowed off and the meat is ground to a flour pictured in the center, then cooking it into a paste to the right.

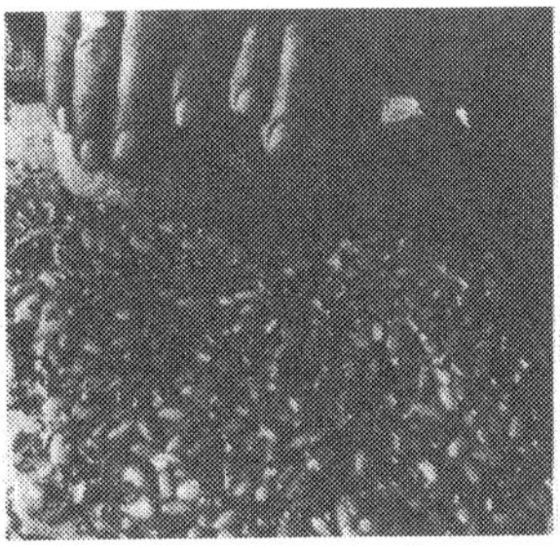

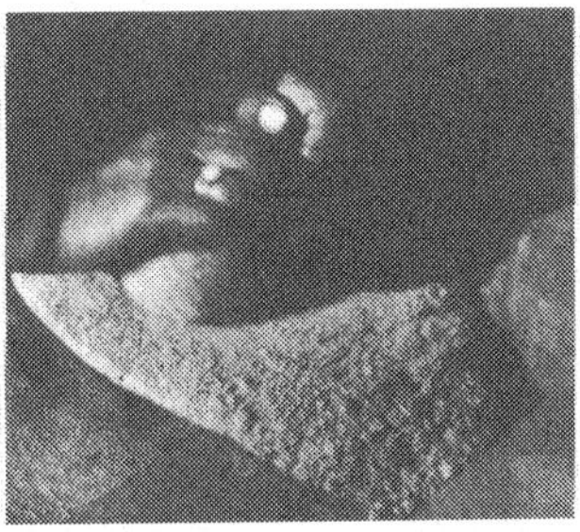

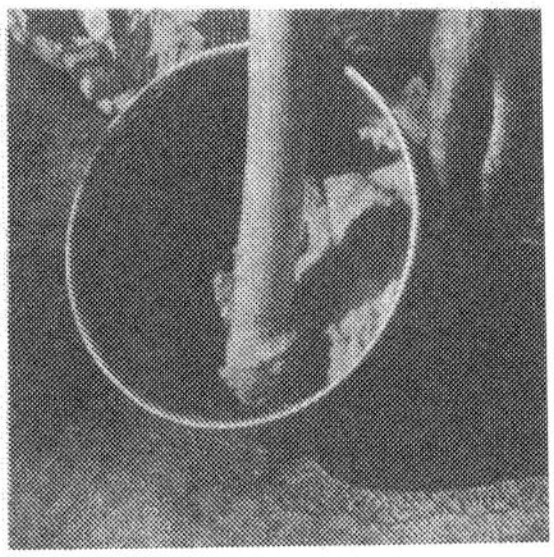

Pictured to the left are caterpillars of the Pandora Sphinx Moth.

The Pandora caterpillars would be collected and stored alive in baskets like the one pictured at the bottom right. This style of basket was also used for grass-hoppers and other insects.

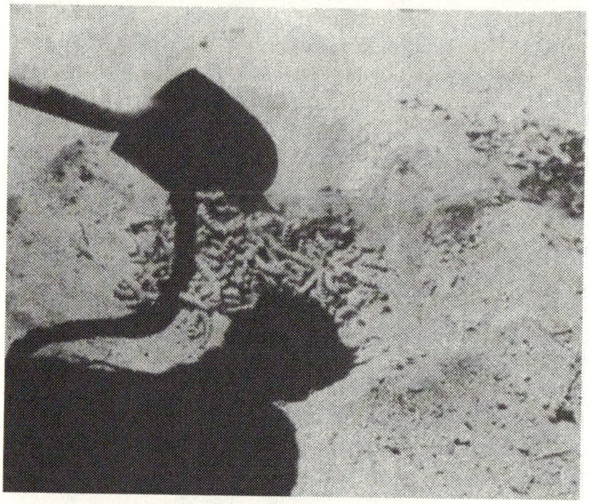

Picture with the shovel is how the cater-pillars are cooked, in sand heated from a fire built on top then cleaned with the sieve pictured at the top left. Then the Pandora Caterpillars are prepared for consumption by boiling them for nearly an hour.

The Pandora caterpillars after being boiled and dried could be stored for several months in a storage shed such as the one pictured at the bottom left.

The Bow and Arrows used by the Washoe

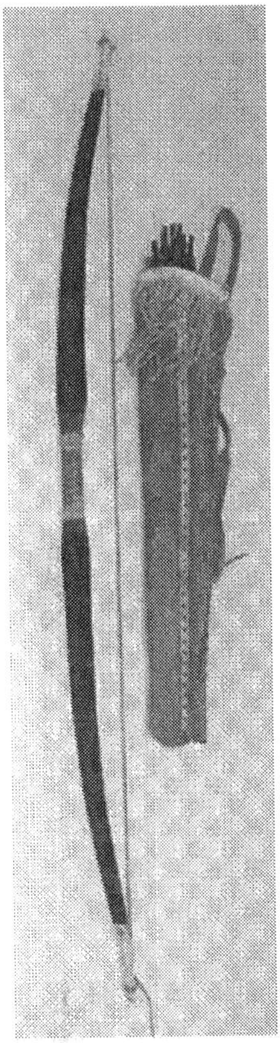

The bow may seem to some to be a rather simple invention but this is hardly the case in regards to the bow used by the Washoe.

The Washoe used a form of the Pandak style bow commonly called a flat bow. These were typically made of Juniper but several other woods could be used. This was backed with sinew, the sinew of ante-lope being considered superior to that of deer but both were utilized. By backing their bows with sinew the return speed of the bow is greatly enhanced, this is a tremendous example of "carbon Fiber Technology" used by the Washoe.

The power of the bow was more a factor of the arrow head toxin tech-nology than anything else. I say this because I have seen Pandak bows that are incredibly powerful yet I read that these people were incompe-tent or weaklings because they used bows of such low energy that a child could pull them back. These analysis were made without a true understanding of what was actually being done.

The typical arrowhead size for this region was rather standard rela-tive to the rest of the world until sometime between 200 and 400 BC. It was in this time period that a new technology was brought into use by either the ancestors of the Pomo or Maidu people. It was in this period that the "Bird Points" appeared, their use was a mystery until only a few years ago: At that time I was working at the Institute of Forest Genetics with recombinant DNA for developing insect pheromones to combat several species of pine and fir beetles.

(continued on page 37)

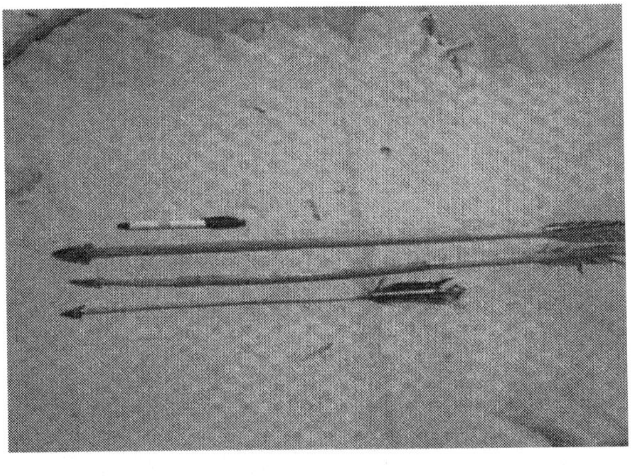

Pictured above a Pandak style Flat bow and quiver. Pictured to the left an Osage arrow with conventional head and shaft, below it a ninety year old "Bird Point" equipped with a detachable foreshaft arrow used by Washoe and Maidu people, below that the very small Bird Point equipped conventional arrow also used by Washoe and Maidu people.

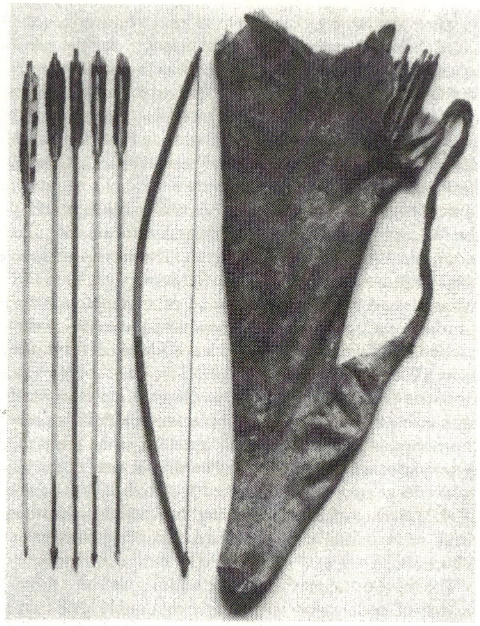

Pictured above a classic bow with arrows and quiver. To the right a man uses a stone of the type pictured bottom left to straighten arrow shafts.

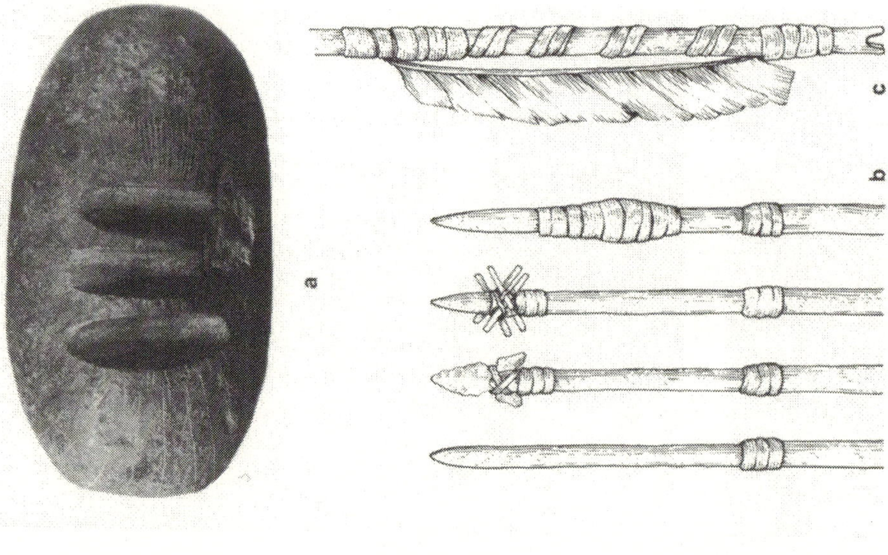

Pictured above Jack Stewart of Big Pine, California. To the left, in 1927 he demonstrates the traditional shooting style with his Pandak bow.

Above to the right Jack demonstrates the use of a fire drill.

Pictured above a Pomo man in traditional battle armor with his pandak style flat bow, typical of many tribes. The conception that California tribes were peaceful is probably due to the fact that their populations were just recovering from the effects of a massive flood in 1543 that had decimated the population. Warfare and armor were just as well developed as the bow and arrow technologies. The armor was made of willow shoots twinned in two layers, the inner being horizontal while the outer vertical. This armor would stop an arrow point from penetrating to the skin yet was light enough to wear. This technology and old tales indicate that California prior to 1543 was a land of extensive tribal warfare much like the tribes in the South Eastern United States.

Pictured above and below the author with a blacktail buck taken with Osage style flint arrow heads, left wing Turkey feather fletching by using an Osage bow backed with deer sinew. One arrow was broken off inside the deer at the depth of penetration when the animal rolled over.

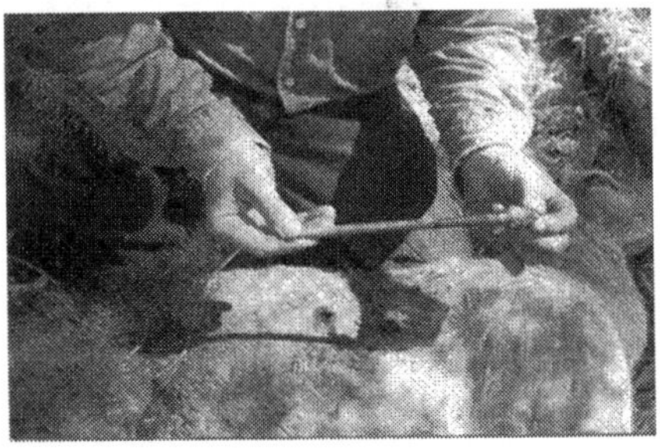

It was while working there that I first heard one of the Entomologists talk about a new project he was working on. It seemed that some of the bird point arrows in several museum's collections had a residue on them that was found to be some sort of enzyme based neurotoxin that had DNA in it from an insect. In his research he found that it was neurotoxin from the Pholcidae, one of the spiders we commonly lump into the term Daddy Longlegs. It seems that those "Ignorant Witch Doctors" had found a way to extract the venom from the Daddy Long Legs spiders. refine and stabilize the poison. What was of financial interest to the pharmaceutical companies was just how these "Ignorant Savages" had managed to preserve these enzyme based neuro toxins. The issue is that all enzyme based medicines and compounds will degrade in a matter of hours or days yet, with all our modern technology, we cannot duplicate the Biochemical Engineers working for the Maidu 2200 years ago. If you were to puncture your skin with one of these 200 plus year old arrows from the museum you have about 4 to 6 minutes before you will assume room temperature. The animals meat would be safe to eat and dangerous animals such as Grizzly bears could be reliably and more quickly killed. It was fascinating to listen to these scientists talk at lunch about how they were now all interested in questioning Maidu and Pomo shamans in the hope that they might be able to figure out this lost technology.

Below is an example of a "Bird Point" Arrow head.

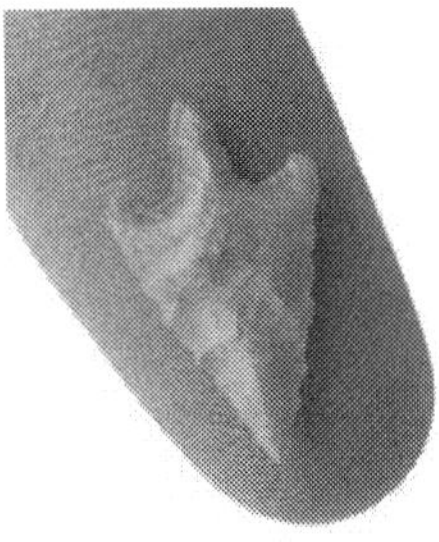

Pictured above are examples of stone arrow heads. Top the detachable Bird point fore shaft, middle the small conven-tional arrow equipped with the Bird point, Bottom an Osage Tribe style conventional stone point (standard for hemor-ragic wounds) comparable to the rest of the worlds arrow heads in size.

The point is that if you are killing big game animals without this technology you will need to kill them by means of a hemorrhagic wound. This requires a powerful bow to drive a large ar-row, tipped with an arrowhead about 3/4 of an inch wide, past the ribs and into the animals lungs; however, with poison arrow technology the idea is completely different. The bird point is a small point not designed to create a large hemorrhagic wound but instead create a small wound the game animal may not even notice and get the neurotoxin into the blood stream.

To do this you do not want a powerful bow. That a more powerful Pandak bow could be made is proven by the Yahoo Tribe. Their arrow heads are the typical 3/4 of an inch wide and their Pandak bows are much more powerful. This was primarily because the species of Daddy Long-legs used by the Maidu, Washoe, Pomo and Miwok is not native to their homeland. In trout fishing in the Maidu homeland creeks like Pull Pull Mull (Weber Creek) and Rock Creek I have found the Pholcidae spiders hanging in clumps and wisps which would be very easy to collect. However in fishing Deer Creek, the heart of the Yahoo Homeland, the vegetation is completely different and there are no Pholcidae spiders. It is my hypothesis that without access to this neurotoxin the Yahi had to use conventional arrow heads and so needed stronger Pandak Bows.

The Washoe used the Pandak style bow and the "Bird Point" arrow heads but the majority of their homeland is too high in elevation for Pholcidae spiders; However, the Washoe were very close trading partners with the Hill Nisenan who did have this neuro toxin. I have also heard but I don't believe there are any surviving examples in any museums of the Washoe using rattle-snake venom on their arrow heads.

Rattlesnake venom is made of highly concentrated digestional enzymes that break down proteins such a heart mus-cles and blood vessels, so it would make sense that if you had the technology to stabilize enzyme based toxins for Pholcidae spiders you could adapt it for using Rattlesnake venom. It is also a good choice as Rattle Snake venom is safe to eat (not that I recommend it) and would not poison the meat of an animal that had been killed with it.

The poison arrows used are of two types: one is a small arrow that is very short but otherwise conven-tional. the other is a normal length two part arrow that is equipped with a short foreshaft with the "Bird Point" that is inserted into the larger primary shaft with the fletching. This system had the Bird Point go into the animal then the primary shaft falls off for the hunter to then pick up and reload with another Bird Point equipped foreshaft. Now another element to this is the fletching or feathers on the tail of the arrow.

These were set on the shaft with the helical twist being achieved by using only feathers from ei-ther a right or left wing. As to which wing side to fletch the arrow depended on the shooter. As it is desirable for the arrow once released to rotate away from the handle of the bow a right handed person would have their arrows fletched with the feathers from birds left wings while a left handed person would use feathers from birds right wing.

Pictured below the Author at Syhylim Toma with his Sinew Backed Osage Bow and examples of the different types of arrow and Stone point technologies.

This is meant to show that the Washoe's bow and arrows were more of a technological marvel than a simplistic, primitive tool.

Washoe Religion, the Shaman

I thought it was better to put this after the description of the Neurotoxin and "Bird Point" technology section. Today most people think of Native American Shamans as "Witch Doctors" with wonderful cures or just a bunch of primitive "Quacks" practicing voodoo.

Wild Parsnip

The Washoe had Shamans but they were specialized technicians. In order to become a Shaman a Washoe Man or Woman had to apprentice themselves for five years or more. This was no small spur of the moment choice.

Pictured above on left a spear point then center and right are obsidian knives.

Shamans were specialists, by this I mean those who worked to create Neuro Toxin for arrow-heads were not medical professionals. Those Shamans who delivered babies were not necessarily the shamans who cured diseases. It is better to think of Washoe Shamans as professionals who were paid for technological specialties. That the religion was a part of this is not necessarily true. By this I mean there were Shamans who were religious professionals much like a cardinal or preacher, they had studied religion not birthing babies or making toxic arrow heads.

Death Camas

There were many plants, insects and other materials that were relegated for use by Shamans only; for example, Wild Parsnips and Death Camas were only used for poison and at certain religious rituals.

For a better understanding of this, often the best stone tool makers were referred to as Shamans simply because it took so many years of training to master this skill.

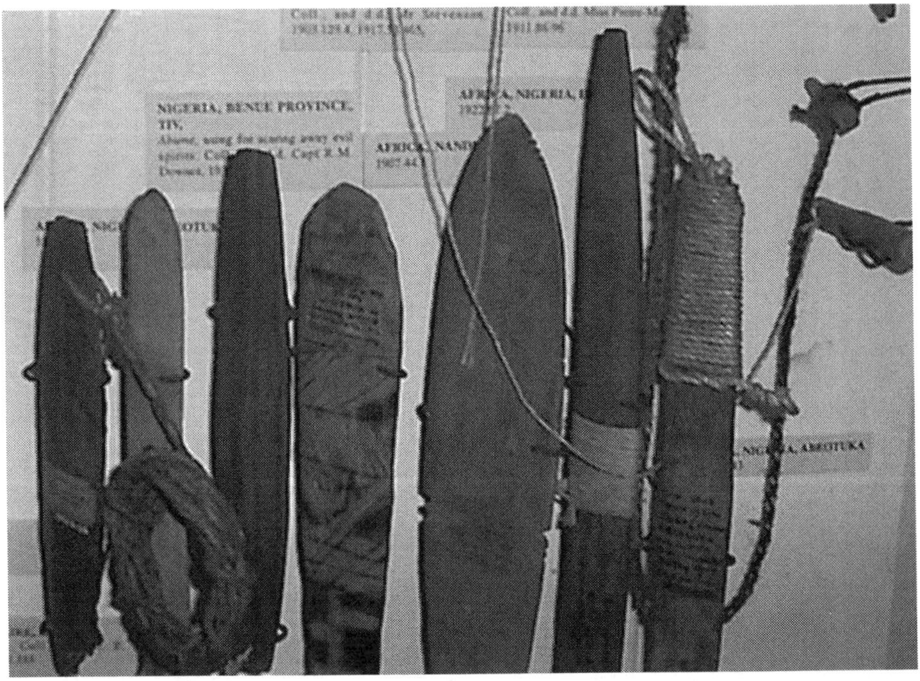

Pictured above are bull roarers. The Washoe Shamans used bull-roarers which when held by the cord and swung around the head produce an incredible, rather unearthly whirring sound. These were used to signal distant people, heal the sick and to bring rain.

Shamans were typically healers and were employed to cure the sick. The Washoe had at least 300 remedies for curing human ailments and some procedures lasted four or more days.

Being a shaman was dangerous, if the shaman was successful they would be paid rather well; however, if the patient got sick immediately afterward or died the shaman was not paid or had to return the payment. If a shaman was determined to be a sorcerer, witch or such they were typically killed.

Pictured to the left the Lady of the Lake at Lake Tahoe, she was believed to have been one of the Lady Shamans who created the Earth.
Pictured to the right a Washoe woman grinds pinyon nuts into flour using traditional tools.

This was my first bear taken with my good friend Buddy and his pack of hounds.

My oldest son Bryan with his first bear.

The Bear (Pano) is a very special animal with great spiritual power. The Washoe religion only allowed men to kill bears and only men were allowed to eat bear meat. The Author's Native American ancestors were members of the Aniga Clan (Bear Clan).

When taking a bear there are certain rituals we observe.

It transcends religion in that it is only honorable to give thanks for the taking of an animal and to treat it and its spirit with respect. That there are certain tribal rituals that are performed in the hunt and cleaning of an animal that is no different from the Jewish system of "Kosher" in dealing with meats. It is not "Savage" to have respect for the animals one hunts and eats, rather it is the opposite. The Washoe ritual for bear is not "primitive religion" and deserves admiration.

Cave Rock (De-ek)

Pictured above De-ek in Washoe Cave Rock located allong Lake Tahoe's East shore.

Located along Lake Tahoe's Eastern Shore, Cave Rock is the most sacred site of the Washoe People.

It is difficult for most Euro-Americans to comprehend this but when a tunnel was bored through Cave Rock in the 1930's the Washoe were appalled in the same way Catholics would be if a tunnel for traffic was bored through the Vatican. At the time the Washoe told them that by doing this, it would anger the "Water Babies", these spirits would extract revenge for this desecration. This was merely laughed at but that year the Truckee River flooded, destroying a great deal of the developments in the Carson Valley.

Then in 1951 another hole was bored through Cave Rock and then again later that year the Truckee River flooded and destroyed even more of the structures in the Carson Valley.

In more recent years a great number of rock climbers began climbing Cave Rock leaving their ropes and pitons. In addition they began painting graffiti all over Cave Rock. To understand the Washoe imagine the same thing being done to the Vatican. After considerable reluctance in 2008, the United States Forest Service finally restricted the rock climbers and removed the bulk of the graffiti from Cave Rock.

Many vacationers feel as though they have been severely restricted and frequently complain about these restrictions but if they were aware of the significance of this site they may better understand the Washoe peoples aversion to these activities.

Pictured below the 1931 tunnel through Cave Rock. To the right a view of Lake Tahoe.

The Cave of the Giant

Cave Rock along the Shore of Lake Tahoe was close to the Giants Cave.

Washoe legend tells of a Giant who lived in a cave (now just under water line) near Cave Rock who would kill those Washoe that strayed near his cave. This legend has several variations but all of them speak of the Giant who lived in that particular cave. Most newly arrived Americans simply dismissed the Washoe legends as fairy tales, however tales of Giants are not limited to the Washoe people.

The Paiute people also have legends about Giants they called the Si Te Cah. The Paiute stories described Red Haired Giants who they said lived along the shores of Lake Lahontan when the Paiute first arrived. They said these giants ate the roots of the tule plants and made rafts from them to move around the water ways.

Sarah Winnemucca Hopkins, daughter of Paiute Chief Winnemucca, on her tours of the East and in her book related many of her people's tales about the Red Haired Giants. However, like the Washoe stories, they said these giants were not above catching a stray Paiute who they would kill, taking the meat and drying it as jerky just like they would a deer or any other animal.

Tule rafts were used by the Giants as well as the Washoe.

Sarah Winnemucca Hopkins in 1883 (Daughter of Pauite Chief Winnemucca of Nevada

Pictured above, explorer and author Stan Nielson has done a lot of the research on the Lovelock Giants.

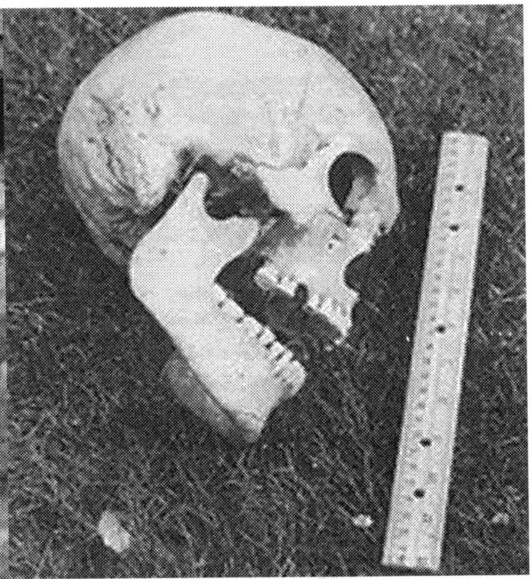

Pictured above a giants skull with a ruler for reference.

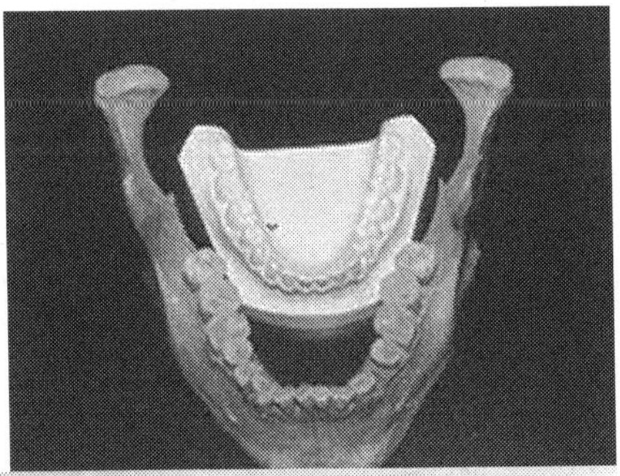

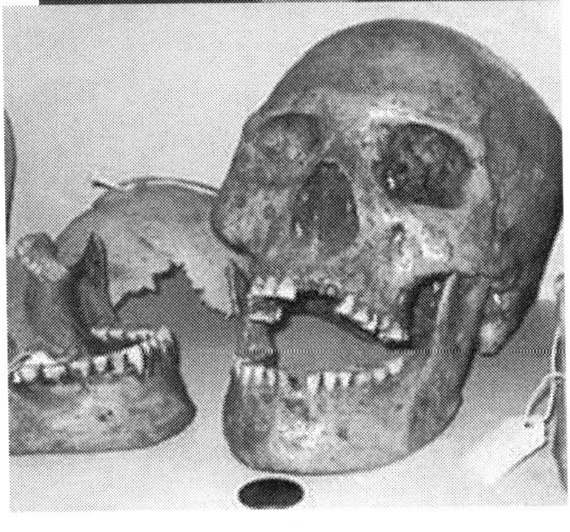

Pictured below right is a giant's skull in the Humboldt Museum at Winnemucca Nevada. To the right is a giants jaw with the impression of a normal persons jaw lying in-

The Paiute stories speak of a war between them and these giants that went on for a long time. One story had a group of these giants living in the Horseshoe Cave near Lovelock Nevada.

The Giants would not come out to fight the Paiute so the Paiute put brush and wood at the entrance of the cave and set fire to it, the Paiute then killed the giants who came out with arrows while those who stayed inside died of smoke inhalation. This story like the others was dismissed as a fairy tale by the American settlers until American Miners began mining the guano from Horseshoe Cave and to their surprise found the mummified remains of the Giant!

News Feature Section

MARCH of EVENTS

Eminent Writers World Topics

WAS THE GARDEN OF EDEN LOCATED IN NEVADA?

Expedition Confirms Finding of Carvings, Possibly Oldest in World

A newspaper from the period of the find played on the sensationalism of the giants.

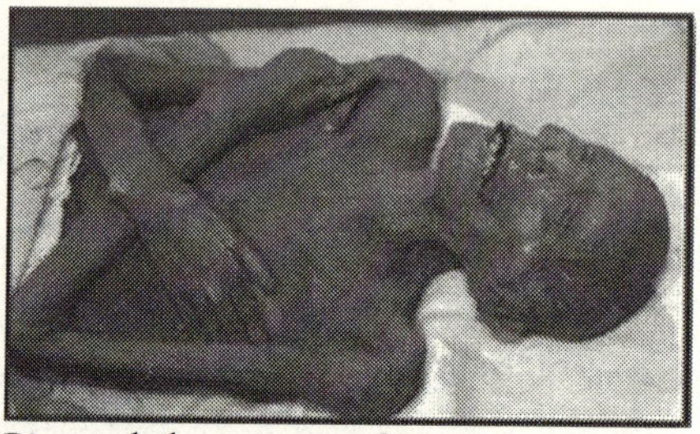

Pictured above is one of 23 giant mummies recovered from the Horseshoe Cave near Lovelock Nevada.

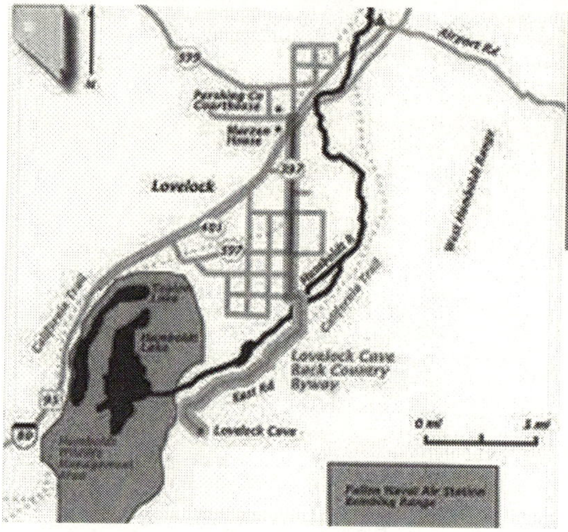

Pictured above is one of the sandals recovered which measures 15 inches long. These giants were proportionately large extremities.

Researchers found that the Paiute story was true! The entrance of the cave had numerous Paiute arrow points in a layer of charcoal and ash. The bodies of the Giants were preserved by the chemical extract from the bat feces (guano).

They found that these people truly were giants with several female skeletons being over seven feet tall and male skeletons ranging from 8 to possibly 12 feet tall. The skeletons were proportionate with the skulls being huge. A sandal recovered from the cave measures 15 inches long. The sandal and a skull as well as other items can be seen at the Humboldt Museum in Winnemucca, Nevada.

Later from 1931 through 1947, near the Humboldt Dry Lake bed, Dr, Bovce and Dr. Russell recovered several more giants remains. One female was 6 feet 5 inches tall and a male was recovered measuring 8 feet 5 inches tall and another male measuring 10 feet tall. As the average Paiute man is only 5 foot 6 inches tall these were indeed giants. Only recently has DNA from these various finds been analyzed to find that these giants did indeed have red hair.

Pictured above is the mummy holding a baby that was recovered by G.F. Martin in 1885 in the Yosemite Valley near Bridal-Vail Falls she stood at least 6 feet 8 inches tall.

The Washoe story about the Giant who lived in the cave by the shore of Lake Tahoe is further confirmed by the tales of the Ahwahneechee of the Yosemite Valley. Their stories spoke of giants they called Oo-el-en who lived in the Valley when they arrived. They also said that these giants would on occasion kill an Ahwahneechee and eat them. Their stories were also called a fairy tale until in 1885 Mr. G.F. Martin was mining in the Yosemite Valley near Bridal-Veil Falls when he noticed carefully stacked stones against a cliff face. He and his crew of miners thought they had found a lost treasure and removed the stacked stones only to find the mummified remains of a woman holding a baby: This woman stood at least 6 feet 8 inches tall!

Many now believe that the majority of the Native American legends of Sasquatch and such are actually rooted in factual accounts of meetings with or sightings of Oxo-el-en or Si-Te-Cah people. The Si Te Cah tribe or tribes had obviously been scattered throughout the region and the Paiute war against them would have caused the surviving members to scatter further as either individuals or small family groups. Due to their large size alone they would have been intimidating to people of smaller stature and due to their experience with the Paiute the Si Te Cah people would have been inclined to be cautious to the extreme. Many now see this as the root of these legends.

However, the Red Haired Giants did not go extinct, as a matter of fact their genetics were distributed over a large region. Recent genetic research has revealed that the New World was initially populated by several races. The first race to discover the New World was actually Australian Aborigines who landed in South America somewhere along the Chilean coast. The Bering Land Bridge from Asia brought populations of Asian and Caucasian peoples and Caucasian seal hunters working along the ice flows also made it to the Eastern coast of North America. These peoples mixed and expanded down into South America where the Australian Aborigines who had landed with a very small population. Mitochondrial DNA reveales that no more than 43 aboriginal females that lived to have offspring made it to South America.

Picture of a family of Ona Indians from Tierra Del Fuego

The Ona tribe of the Tierra Del Fuego region of South America have a large percentage of Australian Aborigine genetics.

As would be expected the mixing of all these different people was not uniform and different tribes and regions had very different characteristics. Even today it soon becomes apparent to most Euro-Americans that Washoe people do not look like Paiute people and they themselves see the differences even more clearly.

Pictured above Osage Chief Black Dog (III) at 6 feet 8 inches tall, who was a close friend of my ancestor Washashot-inga Habashudutsy, it was his great grandfather who stood over seven feet tall who greeted Captain Clark on their expedition.

The genetics of the Si Te Cah people make up a large percentage of my Native American Tribe, the Osage people. As a matter of fact when my ancestor Bill Williams married Acinga Redcorn their two daughters both had red hair. As red hair is a recessive trait you would think that Acinga was part European but in fact she was full blood Osage. It was not uncommon for members of the Osage tribe to have red hair and the average male height was over 6 feet with many going over 7 feet tall. For instance, when Louis and Clark visited the Osage, our Chief Black Dog The First was noted by the expedition to stand well over 7 feet tall. French traders commented that the Osage pulled more powerful bows than any other tribe in the region could, because their men were so large their bows were simply proportionate to their size. This was confirmed by the Lipan Apache who lost the battle of Cutthroat Gap against the Osage who showered the Apache attackers with arrows at such long range the Apache couldn't even get close enough to reach them with their arrows. The Osage men's stature was simply so much larger than the Apache that they could pull back bows far stronger than the Apache. Several skeletons from 8 to 9 feet tall removed from Spiro Mounds, an Osage tribal burial mound in Oklahoma, in the 1930's. These genetics also show up in the populations of Choctaw, Cherokee and Pawnee people to a measurable degree.

Cortez and his men observed Native Americans with red hair and that some stood well over 6 feet tall. So it wasn't that the Si The Cah people were a group of vagrant Vikings, they were simply a part of the North American peoples genetic base. However with a small founding populations and genetic isolation the Si Te Cah of the Lahontan basin became an extreme derivative.

For those who are dubious that humans can get to be so large I think you should be aware of what has been done with selective breeding (an isolated gene pool) in another common mammal species. Starting with the common wild dog we humans have, through isolating a gene pool created the Chihuahua and the English Mastiff.

As an example for a wild dog take the Dingo who weighs in at around 20 or so pounds. If allowed to randomly breed this is the average size of dog. By selecting for certain genetics and isolating them we now have the Chihuahua at 6 pounds and the English Mastiff at 180 pounds.

These are all the same species. The Mastiff being 30 times larger than the Chihuahua!

Pictured above the Wild Dingo at 20 pounds, to the right an English Mastiff at 180 or more pounds while below a Chihuahua at 6 pounds.

Relative to the random breeding example (Dingo) the Chihuahua is 1/3 the size and the Mastiff is 9 times. Applying this to humans living in an isolated gene pool it is possible to have a Si Te Cah tipping the scales at more than 1000 pounds.

The Si Te Cah male mummies and skeletons are ranging from 6 to 10 or more feet tall. The Lummi tribe's Ts'emekwes (Sasquach) was only about 8 feet tall at best. The Native American legends are factual, but it is not some strange ape species they were describing, simply members of a displaced tribe of fellow human beings.

The Coming of the other tribes

Pictured above a California Native Tule Raft

The Washoe were long time residents when the first of the new people began to arrive.

The Washoe and the giant Si Te Cah lived for a long time in the region before any other people arrived. The Si Te Cah were primarily in the Great Basin to the East of the Washoe and while they had almost no interaction with one another there was no real conflict between these two peoples. They simply went about their lives in their own areas and had no interaction, their world changed as new peoples began to arrive. First, the ancestors of the Maidu arrived. They got along well with the Washoe making their homelands to the Washoe's North/ West and intermarried with the Washoe more than any other tribe.

Pictured above a Paiute boat from Pyramid Lake with a big catch of Lahontan Cutthroat Trout Pictured to right the grinding rock at Chaw Se in Amador County California.

Then the Miwok arrived from the South West and the Pit River People from the North East. These people got along fairly well with the Washoe and there was some intermarriage with them. By all accounts from both sides these tribes were not particularly warlike and respected the Washoe's and their territorial boundaries.

None of these new peoples had any real interaction with the Si Te Cah but they were familiar with them and found some Si Te Cah living in their areas from time to time. The Si Te Cah were antisocial to the extreme but there was no real warfare.

It was some time later that the first of the people later known as the Paiute arrived. The Paiute, coming from the East, are a splinter group from the greater Ute tribe, a true Warrior Nation. As they expanded their range into the Great Basin, the Paiute came directly at odds with the Si Te Cah. This resulted in the first real warfare in a tribal sense in the region.

As this war progressed refugee Si Te Cah began to show up in the lands of the Washoe, Miwok and Pit River People as well as further North and West.

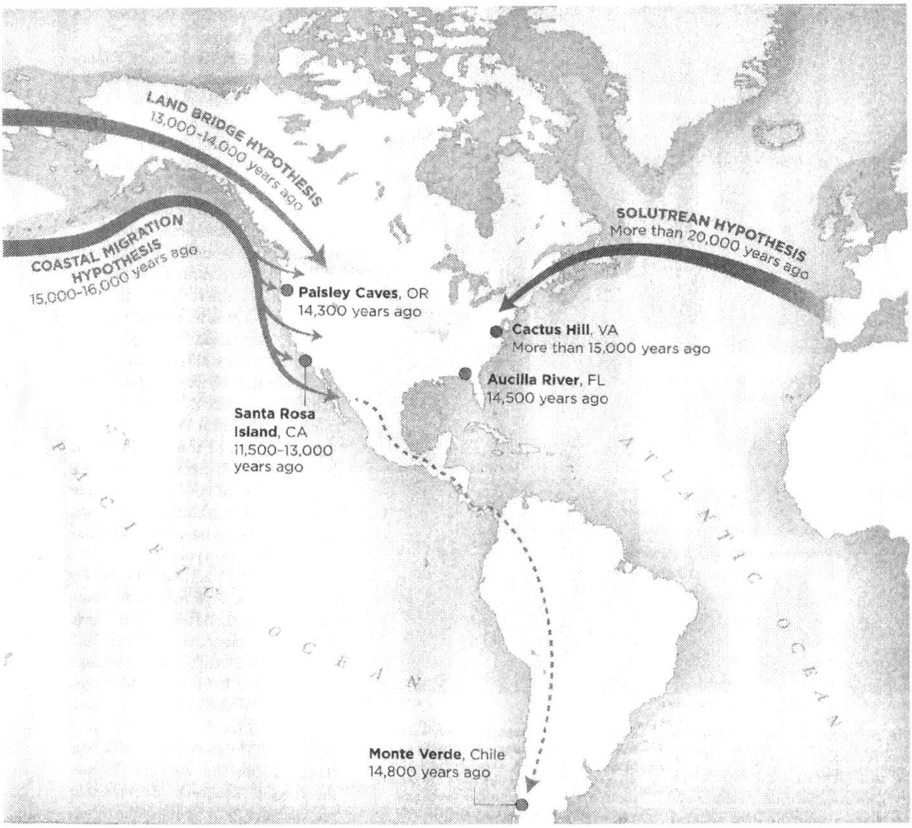

Even this map is now out of date with recent findings since it doesn't show the even earlier arri-val of Australian Aborigines on the Southern coast of Chile. In addition Polynesian peoples also arrived by sea along the Western coast of the Americans, albeit much later than the other migrations.

All of these migrations brought many different racial groups within each of them to the Western Hemisphere over a long period of time. These groups moved about with some mixing with other groups more than others. The Si Te Cah and other similar groups would be expected under such circumstances.

The Washoe settling in the Lake Tahoe Region 9,000 years ago is not surpassing as people had been on the North American Continent for possibly 10,000 years before then. It would be expected for groups who found choice areas to settle in them and take them as a homeland.

Eventually the Paiute drove out or exterminated all the Si Te Cah in the Great Basin. The Paiute were racially very different from the Washoe, Miwok or Maidu but they were interested in trade with these tribes and there was some intermarriage between them.

This community was in place for centuries before the coming of Columbus. When the Spanish explored the Southwest the Washoe heard about it. When the Spanish landed on the coast of California the Washoe heard about it. While they had not seen a white European the Washoe knew a lot about them for centuries.

The arrival of Europeans had little effect on the Washoe until about 1820.

Pictured above Northern Paiute family and pictured to the left a Paiute mother and child.

It was at this time that the Ute Tribe introduced enough horses to the Northern Paiute and they realized the strategic and economic advantages it would give them. The Northern Paiute had been scratching a meager existence out of the Great Basin before this but with the horse they became masters of the land. With enough horses they could battle the Modoc slavers who for centuries had been preying on the Paiute along the present day boundaries of Oregon, California and Idaho. With enough horses the Northern Paiute could expand their access to the natural resources of the Great Basin and their population began to grow. With the realization of just how much the horse could benefit the Paiute people that they began to look for ways to acquire a lot more horses. The Ute tribe was buying horses from the ranchers in New Spain (New Mexico) by trading them for slaves. For the Northern Paiute there was nothing of enough value they could provide the New Mexicans to buy horses except for slaves.

My Ancestors involvement in the Ute horse trade.

It is difficult to realize the scale of the demand for horses to the Ute and Paiute. In my case it is part of my family's history. My Great Great Great Grandfather's Father was "Old" Bill Williams, the Mountain Man. As a young man he had become a member of the Osage Tribe.

While living at the Harmony Mission, Bill Williams translated the Bible into Osage and created the book titled "Osage First Lines of Writing". Later he married an Osage Indian Woman named Acinga Redcorn, they had two daughters while living in Big Osage Town. Their older Daughter named Mary would later marry an Osage Warrior named Yenglenka Nixion, the son of a French Doctor and his Osage wife, their son was my Grandfathers Grandfather, Bill Nixon Redcorn.

After the death of his wife Acinga Redcorn "Old Bill" went to New Mexico where he married the Widow Antonia Baca and they had a son Named Jose Williams. With his new family in Taos he began working with the Ute Indians and became a full member of this tribe.

Pictured above "Old Bill" Williams grandson Bill Nixon Redcorn

At that time the Ute Chief Walkara (Yah-Keera) was the most powerful chief in the region; born of the Timpanogos he had learned to speak English, Spanish as well as seven other Native American Languages. In his rise to power he had created an alliance of tribes in the great Basin whom were keenly aware of the advantages that horses would be to their standard of living. Then in a scheme worked out between Thomas Peg-Leg Smith, Phil Thompson, Levin Mitchel, "Old Bill" Williams and the Ute Chief Walkara, they made the Largest Horse Raid in the history of the West. I guess if your ancestor is remembered as a horse thief, at least mine wasn't considered a PETTY HORSE THIEF. In 1840, these men organized a force of Ute, Paiute, Shoshoni and Bannock to go into Southern Cali-fornia where, with the willing help of the enslaved Mission Indians, they rounded up an estimated 6,000 horses from the Catholic Missions at San Luis Obispo and San Juan Capistrano, then drove them over the Cajon Pass into the Mojave Desert. Once over the Mountains the majority were taken on the Old Spanish Trail into what is today Utah while smaller groups splintered off going North into Nevada. My ancestor "Old Bill", with some Ute

Pictured above Ute Chief Walkara (Yah-Keera) Translated as Hawk 1808-1855 born as Pan-a-Carre Quinker son of Timpanogos Chief who rose to be the primary chief of the majority of tribes in the Great Basin.

friends, waited for the pursuing Spanish Dons at a spring along the trail on the East side of Cajon Pass. When the pursuers arrived at the spring they dismounted to stretch their legs. As these men walked about "Old Bill" and his Ute friends, dressed as vaqueros, eased out of the tall reeds then quietly mounted their horses riding off to the stunned Dons dismay. There was an exchange of insults that only left the Dons standing in the dust of their horses as "Old Bill" and his Utes rode off, leaving the Dons to walk back over Cajon Pass in their fancy riding boots.

As involved as my ancestor was in this and other similar operations it is no wonder that he was considered a full member of the Ute Tribe. That this one opera-tion acquired 6,000 horses is incredible but you must realize this was only a fraction of the total horse influx into the Great Basin. The Great Basin is the largest contiguous watershed area (water goes in, it doesn't go out) in North America and includes almost all of Nevada and parts of Utah, California, Idaho. Wyoming and Oregon.

Old Bill was a religious man and while he had grown up in Missouri, which did practice slavery, he did not like It and felt in part that the raid for horses on the Catholic Missions in California was justified for two reasons: First, the raid allowed at least some of the enslaved Indians to escape their miserable existence as the Dons would have the horsepower to round them up: Secondly, the horses they brought to the people in the Great Basin would save the lives of many from being sold as slaves to the Mexican Ranchos and Catholic Church owned mines in Chihuahua and Sonora where they were worked to death.

During his life "Old Bill" came into contact with nearly all the tribes of the Great Basin as well as Eastern California (ranging from the Yana and Modoc to the Washoe and Maidu. He traded with them and in the main had little trouble with any of them. To him these were people same as anybody else.

My ancestor was later sought out and hired by Mr. Fremont in 1848. Fremont wanted "Old Bill" to help his government survey team find a possible railroad grade through the Sangre de Cristo Mountains in November. "Old Bill" told him it was foolish to try this in winter but Fremont insisted and the expe-dition ended in a disaster with 10 men freezing to death.

Chief Walkara continued acquiring horses and trading. In 1849 Walkara invited Mormon President Brigham Young to send a group of Mormons to set up a trading post in the Sanpitch Valley in present day Sanpete County Utah. In the brutal winter of 1850 the Ute helped the Mormons bring supplies in by sled over the snow. Later

Pictured below Paiute helping the Curtis survey of the Humbolt Sink of present day Nevada.

in the 1850's the Mormons became alarmed at the Native American slave trade that Chief Walkara and the Utes were operating. This eventually turned into the "Walker War" which ended after Chief Walkara negotiated a treaty with Brigham Young and the Mormons. Walkara later died in 1855 at the age of 50. He was given an elaborate funeral and had a large burial mound with the assets necessary for the three days it would take for his spirit to go. This mound was later robbed in 1906 but Walkara's body had already been removed years before by two of his brothers and several Mormon elders. They had taken it to the ancestral burial site higher up in the mountains to be with the remains of his Father and grandfathers. Toward the end of his life Chief Walkara's erratic behavior caused many people, including Bill Williams, to stop associating with him, Some historians feel he exhibited symptoms of tertiary syphilis.

In 1849 Bill Williams at the age of 62 returned to Taos where he got supplies and triedmto return to the Fremont Party only to be killed in an ambush by Utes. The Utes apologized to his widow Antonia and his son Jose Williams. The Utes took Old Bill's body, giving him a chief's funeral and burial.

Few books let alone the general public have any idea of the scale of this trade and how it shaped the history and peoples of the Great Basin and California. It is largely because this is a part of my families history that I have studied it and its ramifications to this extent.

For the Northern Paiute there was nothing of enough value they could provide to the New Mexicans to buy horses except for slaves.

This was the economic reason why about 1820 Paiute Chief Managa The First officially declared war upon the Washoe, to enslave them and trade them for horses. (For the purposes of keeping it clear there were three Chiefs of the Northern Paiute named Namaga that are historical and this was the earliest one, so I call him Chief Namaga The First, not that he was known to anybody else by that designation)

The horse mounted Paiute swept in on the Washoe winter villages (galais dungals) in the Carson Valley with devastating effect. The Washoe were gathered up wholesale and marched of to lives of slavery in New Mexico. This Washoe—Paiute War continued from approximately 1820 to 1860 when the Paiute finally conquered the Washoe.

Pictured above Northern Paiute Chief Namaga the Second.

The affects of this War were catastrophic for the Washoe. Due to the Paiute's use of the horse the Washoe had to abandon all the areas of their homeland that were open and level enough to give the horse mounted Paiute the advantage.

This War affected the Washoe in many ways. It was the Wel Mel Ti band of the Washoe who had their winter village at Donner Lake when the Donner Party got stranded there. It was these Washoe who actually brought food to the starving Donner party in the winter of 1846-47 until they had only enough food for themselves. When they saw that the Donner Party was eating people they decided to stay away from them. It has been questioned why these Washoe were wintering at such a high elevation, the reason is they were safe from the Paiute. Few historians take into account the "Indians" history and problems. Once you realize what was happening in their world many of these "questions" are easily understood.

Pictured below a group of Mounted Northern Paiute

Pictured above a Washoe winter Home (Galais dungal)

Pictured above Washoe Baskets.

Many Washoe tried having their winter camps at higher elevations, others moved South to the Hot Springs near Earleville where the rough country and loose stone deterred the Paiute as their horses would not be able to run and their advantage would be lost. Still other Washoe moved their winter villages West, down into the foothills to Pleasant Valley and the Traverse Creek Drainage on the Georgetown Divide.

For those Washoe who went down to Pleasant Valley the refuge was short lived. Pleasant Valley had been a region where the Maidu, Miwok and Washoe tribes bordered one another. The trading center of To Go No (today's Sly Park) had been a large commercial hub for thousands of years and was only a few miles East of Pleasant Valley. It was here at Pleasant Valley that a World War started by Emperor Napoleon would devastate the Washoe people.

When Emperor Napoleon Bonaparte invaded Spain and placed his brother on the Spanish Throne he caused a set of events that would have terrible consequences for the Washoe.

From the Roman times Spain was the only source of Mercury in Europe. At the time mercury was essential in the manufacture of munitions and certain instruments. With the mercury mines in the hands of Napoleon's France, England and her allies had to find another source of mercury. After a world wide search the richest deposits of mercury containing cinnabar were found in the hills south of present day San Jose, California. To acquire this source of mercury the British Empire considered invading California. As Mexico had only recently gained independence and was plagued by revolutions it was an easy mark; for example, the Mexican Dictator Santa Anna took by revolution the post of Dictator of Mexico 11 times!

Pictured below Washoe at the Hot springs

But weak as the Mexican hold on California was the British did not have the troops necessary to mount even a modest invasion force.

The Chinese Government had demanded that all Chinese goods be paid for with silver. This caused such a trade imbalance that the British East India Trading Company found that the only way to get that much silver was to produce Opium in India which they then sold to Chinese drug gangs for Chinese silver, this in turn was used to buy Chinese goods to take back to England. This caused an epidemic of illegal drug use in China to the point that in 1839, the Chinese Authorities captured 20,000 chests and another 2.6 million pounds of Opium and destroyed it. In turn the East India Company tried to seize Chinese goods to recover the cost of the opium and so started the First Opium War. This quickly went well beyond what the East India Company's Troops could handle and additional Crown Troops were called in.

Then in another theatre of the world the East India Trading Company had been acquiring more and more of India to increase the production of opium, threatening the Portuguese, who had several colonies in Western India. It so happened that the Portuguese Governor of Goa (Portuguese India), Bernardo Peres da Silva, was the first and only Governor in the 451 years of Goa being a Portuguese Colony to be of Native India Indian decent. He was appalled at the British capture of the small independent Indian States. At the time the Governor of Goa had authority over not only the

Portuguese Colonies in India but South Eastern Africa as well. To stop the British in India Bernardo authorized the sale of firearms to the African natives from their colony in Mozambique to occupy British troops and prevent expansion in India. Bernardo was later reprimanded for this as the Portuguese needed British troops in Portugal to defend against an invasion by Napoleon's Army from Spain. The Portuguese Colony from which the firearms were sold was on the Southeast end of the Continent of Africa, very near the British Cape Colony. The Cape Colony was essential for the British to supply ships going to or from China and India. To make matters worse for the British a young African man named Shaka had taken over his father's tribe the Zulu. He then began expanding their homeland from an area of only 10 square miles to an area larger than that of England France, Spain, Germany, and the Netherlands combined. With an army of over 250,000 warriors he posed a menace to the Cape Colony but now with the possibility of his army being armed with firearms the British were forced to send more and more Crown Troops to the Cape to secure it.

For a more detailed account I have written a book titled Slavery In the West on this subject.

The results of this was that the British had to pay money for the Mercury they needed from California. This caused numerous mercury mining operations to start up in the hills South of San Jose. The problem was that in the final mercury distillation process the workers who did this acquired a lethal mercury exposure after only three to four days of work: While the worker may live for a week to a month, it was a death sentence.

Like most coastal tribes from California to Alaska, the Coast Miwok had always practiced slavery, this had been shifted into high gear as the Missions and Ranchos were willing to pay for Indian slaves. The Plains Miwok (those bands living the Northern San Joaquin Valley) who had been taking slaves for sale to their Coastal Miwok brethren were now catching slaves for sale to the Missions and Ranchos that paid them well. The Plains Miwok were now equipped with horses and European goods. With the English now paying very high prices for mercury the need for disposable labor to operate the mercury retorts caused the demand for slaves to go into overdrive.

Captain Sutter a local example of Indian Slavery for the Native People

Many historians think of the Washoe as being uninformed or little informed about the Spanish-Mexican period in California. the opposite was true. On the border of the Washoe's closest allies, the Nisenan, was Sutter's Fort (present day Sacramento California).

Captain Jonathan August Sutter came to California in 1839 and in 1840 got Mexican Citizenship and a land grant of 50,000 acres where the City of Sacramento is today.

Sutter named his post New Helvetia, or New Switzerland. He had brought some Hawaiian men with him called Kanakas and began building a post that included a fort, distillery, tannery, hat factory and blanket making shop. From his Kanakas and trusted Indians Sutter formed an army of 150 infantrymen and 50 cavalrymen dressed in green and blue uniforms led by white officers who gave them commands in German. This was all made possible by a labor force of between 600 and 800 Indian slaves. These local Indians were forced to work in exchange for food and clothing. A passing American complained of them being fed from horse troughs in the hot sun like animals. If they tried to escape they were whipped, jailed or executed. When a number of them died of disease Sutter had his army go out and capture more "Wild Indians" to make up for his losses. Southern States had laws that made slave-owners take care of old and incapacitated slaves, Sutter, like most California Dons, simply discarded them.

Captain Sutter's private pleasures were with Indian women, some reportedly as young as 10 years old. Sutter's operations were common knowledge to the Washoe who were probably better informed than most when it came to Spanish-Mexican period operators.

Pictured above is Jim Pepper a Yurok in 1894 with his bow and arrow. His headband was made of redheaded woodpecker scalps.
His arrows have Obsidian Arrow heads from the Washoe.
Pictured below Hupa in 1896 doing their White Deer Dance. In their display of wealth are obsidian blades that came from the Washoe in trade.

The local Maidu must have been terrified when the ogre John Sutter built a sawmill on the south fork of the Ameri-can River at Coloma in 1848.

But John Sutter could have been worse: That is when compared to men such as Jose Maria Amador. In 1837 Amador went into the San Joaquin Valley and lured a group of about 200 Indians across the river for a feast of Pinole and dried meat: Once over the river his men sprang on them capturing them. He separated about 100 Christians from the group and executed them. Then he and an aide baptized the remaining 100 or so Indians and executed them.

Having a county named after Amador would be akin to naming a German State Himler in recognition for his out-standing liquidation of taxpaying citizens with gas chambers and ovens.

Does Sutter actually deserve to have streets, cities schools and hospitals named after him? How does history judge these men? After all the people they killed were only Indians.

Local tribesmen brought news of these activities to the Washoe while tribesmen from the East brought news of events in New Mexico, Colorado and even farther East. For anyone to even think the Washoe were ignorant of news and events beyond the boundaries of their home-land is counter to the fact that the Washoe were situated on the East-West trade routes.

While the Plains Miwok were willing to take some Mountain Miwok as slaves it was preferable to take people who did not speak their language, this brought the slavers to the Northern boundary of the Miwok. They quickly depopulated the area from the Middle Fork of the Cosumnes River North to the South Fork of the American River. Those Maidu people of the Hill Nisenan Band who had been living in this area were taken or fled to villages North of the South Fork of the American River. The Maidu Villages of Onchoma (present day El Dorado), Banak am Mo-luk (Diamond Springs) and Ekelpa Kan (near Placerville) and at least five other villages were abandoned at this time. Those Washoe wintering in Pleasant Valley who had fled from Paiute slavers were rounded up and taken as well. Only the Village of To Go No (Sly Park) remained inhabited primarily due to how far East it was and because of it's elevation. There at To Go No Mountain Miwok, Maidu and Washoe did continue to winter together for twenty more years.

Pictured below Northern Paiute

For those Washoe who had gone to winter on the Georgetown Divide, their oldest friends the Hill Nissenan Band of the Maidu, gave them the region along Traverse Creek to spend their winters.

It was here along Traverse Creek that a Hill Nisenan man married a Washoe woman and had a son who would later acquire the name Coppa Hembo (Grizzly Bear Killer). This union was not unusual as there had been more intermarriages between the Maidu and Washoe than the Washoe had with any other tribe.

Pictured above: the Author overlooking one of the Washoe Refugee camps provided for the Washoe by the Hill Nisenan along Traverse Creek in the serpentine belt near Georgetown, California.

It was some twenty years later, in the fall of 1848, that Miwok slavers would mount an expedition across the South Fork of the American River to attack the Hill Nisenan Village of Syhylim-Toma (Mosquito) and three other villages in that vicinity. The slavers were observed by Hill Nissenan sentries and the information about the attack sent by "Singing Stones" (a bedrock system that used a tapped code to transmit messages through the bedrock formations from one area to another) to the principal Village of the Hill Nisenan called No Po Chitta Toma (located near where Kelsey is today).

Here the Chief (huuk) later named Captain Juan, sent his oldest son Tucumbo,

Pictured above Chief (Huuk) Coppa Hembo was a mixed blood, his mother was Washoe while his father a Hill Nisenan. His outstanding leader-ship raised him to be a (Huuk) Chief of the Hill Nisenan.

The Author standing under the Grey Eagle Oak where Coppa Hembo's father and mother, legend says, met. Located on the primary trail leading from the Washoe (dungals) villages located along Traverse Creek going to Lake Tahoe.

Coppa Hembo and many of his warriors to attack the invaders. By a system of singing stones and messengers many Hill Nisenan and Washoe villages heard about the attack and sent warriors to fight. The Battle culminated in Rock Creek Canyon with considerable losses on both sides including the primary Chief's son Tucumbo being killed. Coppa Hembo commanded the force of Hill Nisenan, Washoe and Washoe—Hill Nisenan mixed bloods against the Plains Miwok slavers: defeating the invaders and driving them back across the South Fork of the American River (Natoman). For more about this and the institution of slavery relative to Native Americans, I go into it in great detail in my book "Slavery In the West".

Pictured above Castle Rock the vantage point from which the Washoe and Maidu scouts ob-served the slavers invading and transmitted the information by this "Singing Stone" formation North to Nopochitta Toma.

Because of his courage and presence Coppa Hembo would rise to be the primary Chief of the hill Nisenan Band of the Maidu and those Washoe living on the Georgetown Divide. It was Coppa Hembo who in 1851 asked Richard Steel to show the Maidu how to vaccinate against small pox. Coppa Hembo then orchestrated a vaccination campaign that vaccinated nearly all the Hill Nisenan and Washoe living on the Divide (some 2400 people) and many of those Washoe who were living around Lake Tahoe, including his much younger cousin Gumalanga (Captain Jim).

Pictured below the Author at the grinding mortars to the Village of Syhylim Toma

Coppa Hembo had his people help build the first two elementary schools in El Dorado

Pictured below a "Singing Stone" Om-Blu-Kai-oo

County and by his actions managed to have the Native American children integrated into the public schools on the Georgetown Divide from the very beginning in 1852. This integration was very successful for his people as they were not rounded up and sent to either the Round Valley Reservation, as the northern Maidu were (see the Maidu Trail of Tears), nor were his people segregated to local limited reservations. They had numerous small rancherias and were able to fully integrate into American society.

His legacy was a level of racial tolerance that was 130 years ahead of the rest of the Nation. If you want to know more about Coppa Hembo I have written a biography on him titled "A River Divided The Story and Biography of Coppa Hembo".

For those Washoe living around Lake Tahoe the flood of Gold Miners in 1849, went right through their trails both to the North and South but not through their beloved Lake Tahoe.

Pictured above Honey Lake

At this time a man named Joseph Grey moved to Lake Tahoe and built a cabin along the lakeshore. Joseph enjoyed the Washoe's company and bought extra supplies of food to feed the Washoe so that they would keep him company through the winters. This was a godsend for the Washoe as here they were safe from the Paiute.

It was the next silver rush to the Comstock lode and the creation of Virginia City and Carson City that would cause nearly the entire resource base of the Washoe to disappear. The demand for wood to fuel the steam engines and lumber for railroad ties and buildings as well as for shoring tunnels consumed the very pinion pine trees the Washoe needed for pine nuts. The miners also brought herds of cattle, sheep, horses, and mules. These animals grazed the very meadows the Washoe had cultivated for thousands of years with over 170 species of plants.

Washoe woman at Tahoe

To the North in the Honey Lake basin things got worse for the Washoe: There the local settlers began to farm the very meadows

Picture below Mono Lake

Pictured above ranchers and miners took to hunting the Blacktail and Mule deer indigenous to the region for food.

and grass lands that had been the sites where the Washoe cultivated 7 species of native grass for their seed to make flour, in their place the settlers planted potatoes. By Washoe custom you shared food with people you meet. To the White settlers this was seen as begging. As the Washoe didn't ride horses they were seen as an inferior group of subhumans to these white settlers. By the winter of 1857 the Washoe were in terrible distress as their pinyon groves were nearly all cut down, the big game shot, and the grass eaten by livestock. They began digging for potatoes in the fields of the Honey Lake Basin.

This "theft" of property was repulsed by the settlers shooting down the Washoe people. This escalated into what became known as the Potato War of 1857.

Pictured below to the right "Chief" John McCook and his companion with a load of deer meat. As the whites moved in many Native people became professional hunters as a way of making a living.

Pictured above two Washoe boys at Lake Tahoe

Few history books even today tell what was happening at this time. To read the accounts written by the settlers of the Honey Lake country during this period you would believe that the Washoe were the worst specimens of subhumanity alive on Earth. The reason for these accounts painting the Washoe in this way was an attempt on the part of the settlers to get state money, this was a standard practice at the time. Of the incredible number of 49ers who came to California to get rich only a very few actually did so. A considerable percentage of those who came were not the most honest individuals to begin with.

The new State of California had only a few Federal US Army units at that time and these were stationed at the port forts. California had declared what became known cumulatively as the Bald Hills War. Starting with the Klamath and Salmon River War of 1855 and the Wintoon War of 1858 the States objective was to open up lands for settlers by first defeating and then removing the Native California Tribes starting with the North Coastal valleys. Militias would run out of money and lay off for a year or more then resume hostilities. The Great Flood of 1862 is what actually ended this series of conflicts.

The US Army found it nearly impossible to find let alone fight Native Americans in the Redwood forests. The Federal Army Officers fresh out of West Point Military Academy could not move, let alone use their artillery, cavalry and infantry units in the tactical maneuvers of Napoleonic Warfare here in California's rugged wilderness. This left the prosecution of these Wars up to the California Volunteers and State or County Militias. These units would organize themselves and then acquire supplies by submitting their bill to the State of California. At the start in 1851 and 1852 alone the State of California Legislature authorized payment of more than 1.1 million dollars to reimburse citizens for Private Military Forays.

As a prime example of just how this often worked take this incident from The First Indian War of El Dorado County. The City of Placerville mustered out a force of men to punish Indians. These men, mostly miners who didn't have any real

Pictured above Native Americans mining gold. Many "Indians" quickly became employed in the new American economy. For their success they were usually the targets of these "Private Military Operations" as it gave a legal excuse to rob and murder them.

good prospects, promptly went up to Cockeyed Jack Johnson's ranch and store (today's Camino on US 50) where they set up camp and began prospecting the area for gold all the while drinking liquor and having their meals at Cockeyed Jacks. After this "rigorous" deployment they submitted their bill for service and despite some grumbling from locals in Placerville, who were aware of the scam, their bill was paid for by the state of California. For many of the unemployed 49ers it was seen as a good way to get provisioned and go prospecting in some new country, all at the taxpayer's expense.

For some bloody minded ones it was a way to get paid for murdering people they could also rob. The Mill Creek Yana in Lassen County were known as hard workers in the farmer's fields and just as soon as the crops were in and the Indians were paid, these "Private Military Units" would show up killing any Yana they could find for the $40 or so, they would have on their person from being paid for the seasons work, and then scalping them to take to the state where they submitted their bill for military services.

The "Settlers" in Honey Lake were not doing very well and used the excuse that Washoe Indians were "stealing their crops" to start a "War" that they could then pin all sorts of "Military Expenses" onto, in the hope that they could submit a Bill to the state for reimbursement. Whether the Washoe actually took any potatoes or not hardly mattered at all, it was an excuse used to make some easy money.

This miserable excuse continued until the spring of 1861 when the American Civil War started. Many unemployed miners joined the Federal Army in California: For some it was patriotism but for others it was a way to get food, clothing and some sure

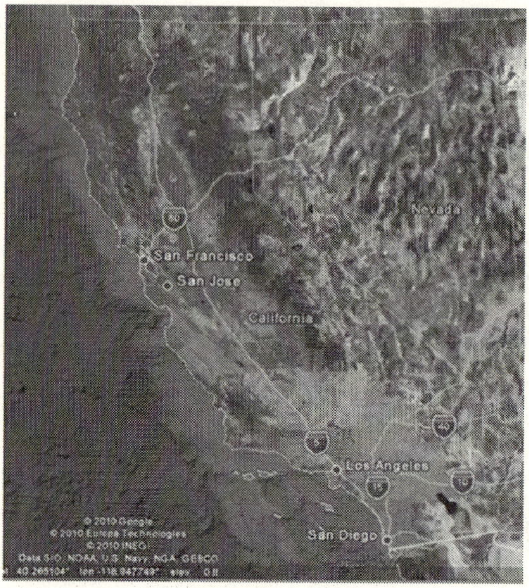

Figure 8. Blue areas indicate ARkStorm flooding as projected by models used in the scenari

Pictured above the California Flood of 1862. Pictured below General Canby

money after losing their stakes looking for gold. Most of these miners believed that they would probably be used in the Bald Hills War where it was highly unlikely that they would ever even see any action.

Then on Christmas Eve it started to rain in California, the rain continued for 43 days. We now know that it was not an "El Nino" but instead an atmospheric river that dumped the equivalent of many Mississippi Rivers into California during the storm. The result was that the State Capitol of Sacramento was flooded under 10 feet of water. The Sacramento and San Juaquin Valleys were turned into a gigantic lake some 30 miles wide and over 200 miles long: over 200,000 head of cattle, 1/2 million pigs as well as huge numbers of sheep, horses and people drowned. Following the flood cholera and many other diseases were rampant. Nearly every fertile valley in California was flooded just as badly. With a near total collapse of the state's economy many more men now volunteered for service in the Union Army. The State of California would be bankrupt for more than two years, not even having the money to pay the governor or legislature let alone the State Militia. The Capitol was moved to San Francisco in large part because it was where food was being shipped in and was still intact after the flood.

The US Federal General Canby was reassigned from California to the New Mexican Territory. For Federal Army units in California they could hardy arrange feed for their horses let alone their men in a state that had nothing: As a result the entire 15 companies of Infantry, 5 companies of Cavalry and single company of Artillery under Colonel Carleton were immediately dispatched for the East to join up with General Canby who had also been reassigned from California to New Mexico.

As a note General Canby's forces who had experience in the Bald Hills War In California as well as all the new recruits were defeated by Confederate forces later in 1862.

The Flood of 1862 and the Owens Valley Paiute War 1862-1863

General James Henry Carlton

The Great 1862 Flood affected nearly everyone in the region and shaped history there as well. The California Flood of 1862 had a terrible impact on the Paiute living in and around Owens Lake. The weather that on the West slope was a massive rain fall caused incredibly heavy snowfall in their country. This caused a nearly catastrophic die off of the deer, antelope and jack rabbits in their homeland, the later snow melt caused such flooding that most of their crops were washed away. The flood also made it impossible for the Miners in Aurora to get wagon's of supplies over the Sierra Nevada from a state that didn't have much of anything at all and it made getting supplies from the East nearly impossible as all the normally dry lake beds were now flooded and covering the wagon roads or at best rendering then axle deep troughs of mud.

The heavy snow fall covered the forage for the miner's cattle who now drove them all the way to the Owens Valley where they now ate the only crops the Paiute had that hadn't already been destroyed by the floods.

The Paiute were now reduced to starvation and began killing the miners cattle to eat. This brought in the US Army to stop the "Indian War".

When the US Army arrived they promptly began chasing the Paiute all over the Owens Valley for five days and had a battle at Bishop Creek on April 6th, 1862 and another Battle at Mayfield Canyon on April 9th, 1862. General James Carlton arrived and assessed that it was pointless to pursue the Paiute up into the canyons and that his army was extremely limited by its own sup-ply of food. let alone feed the prisoners they had taken if the conflict continued They also could not bring in supplies over the mud and snow from Northern California which didn't have the supplies to begin with. He ordered his men to take all the prisoners they could, men, women, and children and to feed and clothe them with the army's supplies. Once he had enough prisoners who understood that he wanted peace with the Paiute and could take them to a location.

These actions caused Paiute Chief Mannawahe to come in to talk with him.

He then sent out runners to the other bands

This lead to Paiute Chief Captain George to come in with over 400 Paiute on May 22 followed by Paiute Chief Captain Dick and his followers shortly afterward bringing the total number of Paiute prisoners to well over 1,000: This left only a few Paiute under Joaquin Jim still at large. General Carleton considered them no real menace to the security of the region, besides which his army and the prisoners were quickly running out of food. He then announced that the war over and took his army and the prisoners South to Tejon where they had supplies brought in from Southern California which had not been as adversely affected by the flood.

Joaquin Jim and the remaining bands of Paiute continued fighting; however, they had never been shown how to maintain their firearms. These were muzzleloading guns that used black powder, when burned black powder residue has very corrosive salts. because of this the corro-sion in several of Joaquin's guns got so bad that their barrels burst when fired, causing several injuries and at least one death. As their weapons degraded their resistance waned and finally on March 12th 1867 they were defeated at the Battle of Rany Springs Canyon.

General Carleton was known as a heroic Indian fighter however he stood out as a man of honor that in carrying out orders he made decisions that resulted in the least loss of life for both sides. Another note about James Henry Carleton is that he was a Major back in May 1859 when he lead K Company of the First Dragoons into the Southern Utah Territory. He and his men arrived at the site of the Mountain Meadows Massacre which had occurred back in Sep-tember 1857 when 120 settlers in a wagon train were massacred. Major Carleton and his men recovered an additional 34 bodies scattered in the area. Major Carleton was very careful in his investigation of the Massacre and put his findings in a Warrant to the Issuance of a Special Re-port to Congress that this massacre was not done by Indians at all but instead by Mormons dressed like Indians. General James Carleton stands out in history as one of the finest examples of a military officer who was first and foremost a man of honesty and a humanitarian.

Picture below from the Round Valley Reservation.

As untrained as these Union Soldiers were, they could not have been supplied in California, as food and such coming from the Eastern United States would first have to run the full length of the Confederate Coast before going all the way to the tip of South America and then the full length of South America, Central America and Baja California before reaching San Francisco.

Pictured above and below are Hula from the Round Valley Reservation.

Add to this the fact that the area of the Federal part of America (the North) had been experiencing crop failures as a result of continued volcanic eruptions in Indonesia and you can see why they just could not supply a Federal Army of any size in California.

For the Indians in California this had a mixed effect. For those who had already been defeated and driven to the Round Valley Reservation (located near Cloverdale California) the results were a disaster. The State of California, now bankrupt, argued that it was the responsibility of the Federal Government to feed the Indians living in this Federal Indian Reservation.

The Federal Government on the other hand countered that it was the State of California who had initiated the Bald Hills War and they should have to pay for the people's needs, besides which they had a Civil War to fight and could not spare the ships necessary to bring what little supplies they had all the way around the Americas just to feed some Indians when they couldn't even feed their own soldiers.

For those Indians who were not in the Round Valley Reservation it meant that those "Private Military Operations" would have to do their "Injun hunting on their own dime". As a result the number of Private Military Operations dropped to almost none from the spring of 1862 on as they could not expect to be reimbursed by the bankrupt state for their operations. It should be noted that those operations that did continue against Native California Peoples had a very different focus: For those Militia men, either of the State of California or a County, who had enlisted for specified periods of time they were now in a very difficult predicament. They were not being paid by their bankrupt state or county nor were they getting food or clothing; however if they left their command they would be termed "deserters" and as such were liable and could be hunted down themselves, and killed for desertion.

For many Federal Union Militias the new objective was to go and find Native Americans to capture and "sell" them to farmers, ranchers, miners or brothels to get the supplies they needed to feed themselves.

Realize that the Emancipation Proclamation did not free slaves held in Union occupied areas and that Indians were not even considered legally "People" under American law until Ponca Chief Standing Bear's Trial in 1879 where Judge Dundy's ruling was based on the dictionary definition of a person as provided by Charles Webster.

Ponca Chief Standing Bear who's trial finally gave Native Americans the legal definition of "persons" in the United States in 1879

While it is strange to think of Union Blue Coats taking slaves to sell during the Civil War here in California it was not limited to the West Coast. The Union Army in New Mexico spent most of its time catching Native Americans to sell just to make a little more money for the duration of the War and furthermore, the owning of Native American Slaves would remain legal there until 1911.

For those who read the accounts of the period and history of the Potato War against the Washoe around Honey Lake it will make more sense once you understand the actual motivations.

Pictured below Washoe Captain Heel who succeeded Deer Dick as headman of the Honey Lake Band.

Pictured below Captain Jim (Gumelana)

For the Washoe this was their lowest point. From a population of about 1,500 people in the year 1700 stretching from Mono Lake in the South to Honey lake in the North they had been reduced to only 500 people by 1866 with no land at all.

In April of 1880 the Washoe leaders Captain Jim, Captain Pete, and Captain Walker sent a petition to Washington to stop the destruction of their lands.

By 1893 Many residents of Douglas County sent a petition to the government to provide for the Welfare of the Washoe that they described as having always been reasonable and helpful people who had never molested any white people.

By this time the bulk of the Washoe were working on ranches and farms, so when the US Government Agent arrived he recorded only 62 Washoe and in his report said that providing a reservation for the Washoe was not necessary as the tribe would soon be extinct!

Then in 1914 Captain Jim and his daughter Sara sent another petition along with a beautiful basket to the White House. The basket was placed in the white house with a special plate under it but there was no response to the petition.

Their basket was put on display in the White House along with other pieces of art.

Pictured to the right Washoe Captain Kelly in 1910 Pictured below Washoe Captain Jim and his daughter, other Washoe present unidentified.

Pictured above and below are turn of the century Washoe camps. Without any official lands for them to settle on they were at the mercy of others and so might have to leave the camp.

However the Washoe did not go extinct. Today they have 5 colonies around Reno Nevada and in 1996 owned 1,071 acres of land with about 812 Washoe actually living on these lands. The tribe operates their own farms and campgrounds as well as a some small businesses. A much larger number of Washoe live nearby on their own private farms and homes in California and Nevada.

Pictured above a Washoe ranchers hay field.

Although not recognized as The Washoe people by the US Government, many Washoe and mixed Washoe-Nisenan and their descendants live on the West side of their former homeland.

Here they were able continue some of their traditional lifestyle well into the 1940's. After the 1950's most of these people were difficult to distinguish from the local citizenry and today live and work in the region but are not officially recognized as either Washoe or Hill Nisenan. The vast majority are not recognized as being Native Americans.

Pictured below Nisenan many of whom were part Washoe managed to continue their traditions on into the 1930's on the Georgetown Divide and near Auburn California. The Hill Nisenan's last "Big Cry at No Po Chitta Toma and Irish Creek near Garden Valley California was in 1908. Their spring "Weda" Bear Dances continuing for a few more years at No Po Chitta Toma until 1943.

The Tankey Nisenan in Auburn California (Auburn Unified Indian Community) continue some traditional celebra-tions even today.

Many people believe there weren't any Native Americans in their area because they don't have any reservations there today. This is not the case. Many of the Rancherias were dissolved by the US Federal Government. Some of the smaller Rancherias were simply delisted, some as late as the 1960's. The people there were told they were no longer considered Indians.

Other Rancherias were forced to be abandoned and the people relocated to other lands or consolidated on larger Rancherias or reservations. What makes this so confusing is that the Reservations or Rancherias were established by many different authorities at different times.

Pictured below Cupeno Indians camp on Pauma Ranch after being evicted from their traditional Rancheria at Warner's Ranch (Agua Caliente) photo by Sawyer 1903.

For some California Tribes, Reservations could have been granted by the Spanish Empire, Mexican Government, Provincial Mexican Authority, A wealthy Don, The Catholic Church, The Nation of California, The State of California, a County in California, a private landowner in California or the US Government.

This was why so many of the smaller Rancherias in California could be dissolved or go unrecognized. The State and local governments often worked at policies that would eliminate these Rancherias for many reasons not the least of which was to increase their Property Tax base. For some of those that had been granted by their County or a Private Landowner the Indians often managed to simply "Prove up On the Land" and acquired a legal title where it was then simply considered "Private Land" and they continued living there but were no longer recognized as being Native American. This had some advantages. Few realize that Native Americans were not Legal Citizens of the United States until 1927.

Pictured above a Maidu or Pomo Rancheria that might be burnt down and leave no evidence of its existence, pictured below a large round house will stand for a long time and be well known which often gave those people a better claim.

Pictured above Paiutes in Washoe County where they managed to get a small Reservation to live on.

For the Paiute and other peoples in the Great Basin it was nearly impossible to fade into the almost non-existent American Society and with no other govern-mental authorities nearly all of their land became US Federal Government owned. For this reason their Reservations were US Federal Indian Reservations.

The issue as to who assigned the reservations origin was rather mute until the idea of Indian Casinos came into popularity. This came into difficulty because of jurisdictional issues concerning the laws.

For instance Rancherias issued by Counties, Private Individuals, or the State were subject to the States Laws: If the State did not allow Gambling then the tribe could not have a Casino on their Rancheria. However if the Tribe had received their Rancheria or Reservation from the US Federal Government, Spanish Empire or Mexican Government before a certain date they were allowed to have a Casino and gambling as that was not against Federal law. This became more convoluted when tribes had Rancherias and or Reservations all adjacent to one another "given" to them by multiple authorities over a number of years. It became a situation where their parking lot could be in one place but the Casino could not. It was not until this was deregulated that the Indian Casino's became widespread.

Pictured above many settlers who came to the West married local Indian women. The women knew the land, people, had connections and wanted to live in the "West". The children of these families often hid their native American ancestry especially after 1907 as the B.I.A law would make it impossible for these people to operate their own farms, ranches and businesses.

Pictured above and below many local Tribes people managed to integrate into the local US Citizenry so that they would not be segregated. In this way they could still live in their ancestral homelands and possibly pursue some of their traditional crafts and sports. It was a tricky line to balance as they did not want to be seen as different.

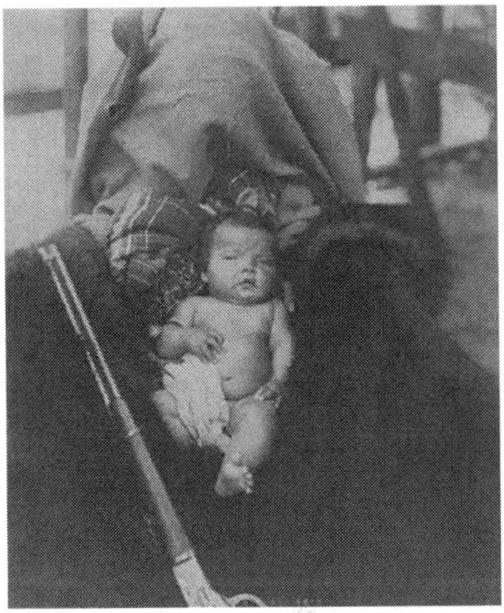

Another factor few Americans realize was that in 1907 the US Bureau of Indian Affairs decided to put out a "Mandate" of sorts that required a person of Native American Ancestry to prove that they had less than half Native American Blood to be considered competent! In an era were few if any people even had a birth certificate this was impossible for even most mixed bloods to prove. If they could not prove that they were less than half Indian they would not receive a "Letter of Compantancy" and as such were not allowed to write checks from their own bank accounts let alone do business without a US Government appointed Guardian to supervise their transactions. By 1907 a great many Native Americans and mixed bloods were businessmen, lawyers, doctors etc. who found this "Mandate" so crippling that many of them moved away and denied their Native American ancestry. Many Native Americans claimed to be Italian or Mexican as a way of explaining their complexion or features to prying US Government officials.

Pictured to the left the Author's Grandparents, Bill and Lois Nixon. Pictured to the right Lois's Father and Isaac's first family was with a Yana Woman and his son George Phillips lived nearby.

It was the 1907 B.I.A legislation that encouraged my Grandfather, after graduating from college, to leave Oklahoma and come to California. The B.I.A. Mandate had made it impossible for his father (my great Grandfather) to operate his own farm on the Osage Indian Reservation. Every time he needed to buy fuel, seed or equipment he had to go find his B.I.A. Guardian to write the check out of his own account. Yet these Government appointed Guardians were not all that honest and as an example, if one of them used an Indian's money to buy a car for a prostitute or anything and the Indian took them to court for mishandling their money it was thrown out of court as the Indian was legally "Incompetent". Because of this both my Great Grandfather, Fred, and Grandfather Bill came to California. Like many other Native Americans from Eastern Tribes they did not stand out as much in California. My Grandfather got a very good job and met my Grandmother who was from an old California Family. Her grandfather had come to California before the gold rush, married a Native Yana Woman, had a family with her and employed her people on his ranch: later he married

Pictured above Lois and her sisters Beatrice and Bernice with one of her father Franks big bucks. Frank and his brothers often went hunting with their half brother George and other Yana kinfolk.

Pictured to the right Lois Phillips parents weddings photo and to the left her parents visit in 1939.

again and had another family that my Grandmother came from. My Grandmother grew up with her uncle George Phillip and his family nearby as well as many local yana (he was a son of her as well as many local Yana pe Grandfather and his Yana Wife) as well as many local Yana people.

Pictured above the authors Grandparents place in 1954. Located in a saddle of the ridge between Spanish Flat and Chicken Flat the Hill Nisenan Rancheria (Hehekeke Toma).

Yet, when my Grandparents went to the Baptist Preacher in Chico California, to get married, he refused and stated' "He would not marry an Injun to a White girl". So they went to the Justice of the Peace and were married.

Pictured below the Author's father Bill with his Aunt Beatrice while she was up visiting her sister Lois Nixon. The two are holding deer fawns that came over to them when called to, the fawns walked back to their mother when set down after the photograph.

After the stock market crash of 1929 the business was taken as well as their home and savings when the bank folded. They and my father then came to the Georgetown Divide. It was unique in several ways. Due to the by then late Chief Coppa Hembo's efforts there was no segregation here. To the North across the North Fork of the American River in Auburn, Indians were not al-lowed to sit with white people in movie theatres and such, while once over on the Georgetown Divide and all the way South to Placerville, there was no restricted seating, or segregation and Indian children were allowed to go to public schools.

Here, my Grandparents set up a saw mill and built a home in the saddle of Shoo Fly Ridge adjacent to the Hill Nisenan Rancheria of Chicken Flat (Hekeke Toma). At the time many of the older Nisenan were still living there and would walk through the saddle in the ridge to go to the settlement of Spanish Flat or on down to my Grandparents saw mill.

Due to the time, location and my Grandparents history they got along very well with all the lo-cals and to their credit remembered the local stories and legends.

Tracking

Pictured above the Authors father nd Grandfather both named Bill.

My Grandfather had an interesting story about a conversation he had with an old Washoe about tracking. This was more of a conversation between two professionals as you might have today between two engineers or doctors. My Grandfather had been born and raised on the Osage Indian Reservation in the Indian Territory and as a teenager had hunted Pronghorn antelope from horseback with his brothers and a couple of friends. They all had Osage bows and arrows but between them only one Cap and Ball Civil War era revolver and one muzzle loading shotgun. For him the art of tracking as it related to the hunt was a science rather than a casual interest. With this in mind it was the techniques used by the Old Washoe that he was interested in.

As I heard the story it seemed that the old Washoe had been talking about some of his wanderings when he was young, telling several other Washoe and other men about narrow escapes and different trips he had made.

Pictured below the Osage drying buffalo meat on their reservation, the Authors Grandfather Bill, remembered his people in a time of transition where the old life style was still being practiced.

It was after the old man had finished his stories and the other men had started to leave that Grandpa came over to the old man and began to ask him pointed questions about certain details the old man had said in his stories. Grandpa didn't remember the stories in as much as he was interested in the old man's tracking techniques. I am going to try to write this the way Grandpa simulated the old Washoe's broken English.

Pictured above a man demonstrates the use of a fire drill.

As best as I can remember the conversation went like this. Grandpa to the old Washoe man, "You were saying that the Paiute tracks you came across were on the run and likely getting away from some trouble to the East. What was it that told you?" The Old Washoe Man said, "A Paiute no walk like a Washoe. Paiute ride horse all time and legs grow different than man who not ride horse so much. Legs bowed some and outside of foot turned in. Even if Paiute wear white man's shoe or boot he walk different because he not have a saddle on his horse like white man does. The tracks was Paiute, and the horses was sweating bad, lots of foam and drips on ground, but land near flat so must have been pushing them hard. Two Paiute piss and blood in it, so they ride very hard. (What fascinated Grandpa and me in his telling was the details that told the Washoe not only who the were but what their condition was. That these men were Paiute was due to the way they walked, that they were in a big hurry was noted because the horses were sweating a lot and the men's urine had noticeable blood in it indicating they had been jolted hard and been riding for some time).

Pictured above White men walk different than a Paiute and their horses have metal shoes. The Old Washoe explained how he knew who they were by the trail they left.

Grandpa then asked the Old Washoe about the lone China Man in context to several Mexicans. The Old Washoe, "I knew it was a lone China Man because even with no shoes he not careful where he step. He walk like kind of drunk white man, all clumsy because of smoke he use." (It was normal at the time for Chinese to use opium and this left them impaired to a noticeable degree in the way they walked. The Old Washoe also used some rather vulgar words to describe that the Chinese diet was reflected in the odor and appearance of their excrement. In determining the race of the person who left tracks, finding their excrement was almost a certain give a way. At the time there was little if any effort made at even concealing let alone covering excrement and as the Old Washoe explained the diet of Paiute, Mexican, Chinese and White were rather different from one another.

Pictured above a woman who has given birth to a child walks differently from one who has not.

The Old Washoe also noted that the urine of a man who had drank whiskey smelled different from that of a man who drank mescal, or tequila, and different still for beer.

The appearance of tobacco spit on the ground was almost certainly a white man while a Marijuana cigarette end was usually a Bolivian. White women wearing shoes with heels and leaving small bottles (laudanum or other painkillers were typically sold in small fashionable bottles) were probably prostitutes. The tracks left by a man are different from those of a woman, Paiute moccasins were very different from Chinese slippers, Irish men's shoes, or Mexican's boots. He also noted that these people all had a typically different style of walking. As an example he said that Mexican's typically walked "like a Buck chicken", they had a strutting style to their walk.

The Old Washoe man also explained how he could tell if the tracks were from a woman who had never had a child or the tracks of a woman who had given birth at some time. Essentially the displacement of the woman's heels is set further apart after giving birth and the orientation relative to the placement of her feet's angle set against her line of travel is very different.

Pictured below, a horse has a very different track from a donkey who is different from a mule's. Even without shoes women walk very differently than men even if their feet are the same size.

He noted that a fat man tends to roll over the outer side of his shoes or boots leaving a shadow mark parallel to the outside edge of his shoe or boot, however a big man who isn't fat doesn't role over the outside of his shoe or boot.

The Old Washoe did say it was difficult even for him to tell the track of a Maidu from those of a Washoe however he could tell a Paiute from a Shoshone because they had different styles of moccasins that left a different print.

Pictured above California Indians on Rancheria in Mendocino County California. The Old Washoe like many in his generation considered the reservations and rancherias a mixed blessing. While they saved the physical lives of those people, they killed the conditions under which the children could study the sciences of nature. The knowledge gained by this education was a large part of what made "true people" and this was being rapidly lost in just one generation.

Then he went into detail as to how he determined the time for when a set of tracks were made. As Grandpa told it, emulating the Old Washoe. "Time tracks made is told by the wind, birds, bugs, and squirrels. Look to see what crawled across the tracks or was stepped on by the tracks. Worms and centipedes move on top at night to avoid the birds, grasshoppers only move late in morning till dusk, oak worms make strings at night to avoid birds while spiders make webs all day and night. Birds, snakes and lizards only leave tracks in the daytime but the birds are early morning while the snakes and lizards are only once the temperature is high enough.

The Grey squirrel doesn't get up to early and doesn't "Dust" his tail until the dust is dry, late morning or afternoon usually. Look for windblown dust in track and think back to when on that day or night the wind blew. On side of mountain wind blows downhill from evening to dawn then uphill from late morning to late afternoon. This coupled with up canyon drafts in the daytime and downdrafts in the evening plus weather events such as strong winds or light to heavy rain, snow or hail. By experience the marks made by light rain versus hail or the amount of debris or grit moved by varying wind strengths and direction. This can only be learned through experience.

I like my Grandfather and Father have been fascinated by this science and by the Old Washoe Man's keen observations and powers of deduction. The art of tracking is a collection of studies, from ability to see patterns in tracks and the minute details of rhythm and style, to the time of day or night determined by all the other creatures actions plus windblown debris and its direction, far from simple it was more like a deduction by Sherlock Holmes. In the study of Nature this Washoe had a PHD, however he was motivated in his studies in a way none of us ever could be, a failing grade in his study meant death.

The Singing Stones / Talking Rocks

Castle Rock

This is a fascinating subject and deserves some more explanation. During the 6000 to 9000 years people have been living in this part of the Sierra Nevada they discovered that some of the bedrock formations run unbroken for miles. Much of these stone formations have a linear grain to them much like wood does. At points where the formation surfaces and the "End Grain" is exposed a person can tap on the stone formation and someone at the other end can hear this tapping.

One such "Singing Stone" formation was demonstrated by Maidu Shaman Rich Adams. The points on the stone formation are 14 miles apart as determined by GPS. The advantage to these Singing Stones is that while sound travels approximately 768 miles per hour through air it travels approximately 3240 miles per hour through stone. In the demonstration people had cell phones at both ends and could hear the distinctive series of taps through the stone with almost no delay from 14 miles away on the cell phone.

During the thousands of years the peoples of the Maidu, Miwok and Washoe tribes lived here they found and set up a network of these singing stones. The terminals were usually manned by either elderly or physically disabled people who had been taught a code. According to witnesses the code was very similar to our Morris code. However without having a written language the code was not carried on to the later generations and has been lost.

As one Singing Stone terminal might not be right next to another it required messengers to re-lay the messages to the next terminal. As an example of this network's capability when it was more or less fully manned we have numerous witnesses dealing with the arrival of Charles Fre-mont's expedition in 1844. Fremont and Kit Carson arrived in the Washoe Homeland and were guided through what is now Carson Pass, High Way 88, Iron Mountain/ Mormon Emi-grant Trail to (To Go No) Sly Park in February 1844. By using the Singing Stones from (To Go No) California Tribesmen as far South as Murphy's California and as far North as No Po Chita Toma (Georgetown California) were aware of their arrival on the same day. The Washoe had heard stories

Pictured to the left K-ocos-oo to the right Om-blu-kai-oo both are Tittii-Tom-oo called singing or talking stones that work much like a telegraph.

about the White Man Kit Carson for years from the peoples in the East, now with his arrival many wanted to see this man. According to several tribesmen who made the trip to see these white men and spoke of it years later they were very impressed with Kit Carson but didn't think too much of Charles Fremont. This does show just how much of a communication system was in place and its relative speed.

About the Author

As an infant my father took me on trips on his old motorcycle down the mule train trails that access some of the most remote parts of California and Nevada. He took me on so many "Expeditions" in his Model T Ford I can't even begin to estimate a number. From the Black Rock of Nevada and the remote canyons to the highest crags he took me following Freemont's trails or old wagon routes.

Both my Father and Grandfather took great pleasure in showing me the details of tracking in pains-taking detail as well as teaching me the wilderness knowledge they possessed.

My father took me on many of his field trips that his work as a Mechanical Engineer he truly enjoys. This took him and by his grace me all over the Western United States. In his work my Father al-ways worked on the principal of attacking the problem and not the people. It was his approach to people that put them at ease with him. At the time I was a boy the United States was building water projects to benefit many remote areas including numerous Indian Reservations. In this way I learned the history of the region from many different sources as I found it fascinating.

My father's view point like that of my Grandfather was from that of a Native American and this was appreciated by all who came in contact with him. Being exposed to the many different points of view I believe was very beneficial to my understanding of the world and history.

It served me well while serving in the US Navy and later while working 16 years for the US Forest Service. With my education and experience I managed to get the job of doing the first abandoned Mine Survey of the El Dorado National Forest. Later I did the first complete survey of all the old Mule Train Trails and later worked as a Forest Protection Officer. As the USFS was not hiring full time employees these were all term appointments and between these I worked for El Dorado County surveying trails in the Lake Tahoe Basin both in California and Nevada.

My appreciation for the land and the Native Tribes has only grown over time. It is my desire to share with you some of this wealth of knowledge.

I would like to share some insight on the late California Grizzly bear.

From my experience and study's in areas still inhabited by Grizzly bears as well as a great deal of experience with black bears I think it might be useful to share some of this with you the reader.

The Grizzly Bear in California was responsible for populations of sea lions and seals being so few that communicable diseases such as distemper were not resident in those animals populations.

The Grizzly forced our local tribes to practice cremation and even caused whole villages to be abandoned. While the extermination of the Grizzly was an extreme measure it may be justified. In their place the Black Bears have now taken over many of the practices of the Grizzly Bear and have multi-plied and thrived. Some Black Bear are just as large or larger than many of the Grizzly bears. While the Black Bear (not always colored black) may look somewhat like a Grizzly they are not the aggressive men-ace that their cousins are. In a state with so many people Black bears have thrived and in-creased in number while those few Grizzly who have come into California have gotten into trouble very quickly.

Pictured above Grizzly bears while below are pictures by the author of a California Black Bear that weighed nearly 600 lbs.

Pictured above a rope and plank bridge for the New River Trail in the Trinity River Canyon photographed by C. Hart Merriam in August 1936. It is implied that this bridge was made by the Chimariko People and that the Maidu made similar ones. Today many of these canyons are still only accessible by old Mule Train bridges or more recent bridges that only accommodate foot traffic. It is still a very remote and rugged landscape few people are aquatinted with.

This picture has fascinated my friend George and I. Having come across the footings to such bridges I couldn't tell if they were from the Gold Rush period or earlier. For my readers let me ask, do any of you know anything about these bridges? I and others would like to know how extensive were they? What was the rope fiber made from? And just how large of an expanse was this bridge. The bridge does not appear in this picture to sag as much as I would think it should when compared to steel cable one's with which I am familiar, are there supporting lines above that are not visible in this picture? A bridge such as this represents a great deal of engineering and resources being expended by anybody let alone the relatively small population of Native American People I would expect from the resources available in an area like this. it is my hope that someone knows more about these Native American bridges? If you do have any information on these questions please feel free to contact me at the address in the back of the book for ordering books from me.

Bibliography

Boule, Mary Null, Native Americans of North America Basin Region, Washoe People, Merryant Publishers, Inc. Vashon, WA 98070 (2000)

Bravo, Leonore M, 1991 Rabbit Skin Blanket Braun Brumfield Inc. USA

Brewer, William H, Up and Down California in 1860-1864 University Press, Los Angeles (2003)

Burrows, Jack. Black Sun of the Miwok, University of New Mexico Press (2000)

California State Military Department (Museum) The California Column and the March to Tucson.

D'Azevedo, Warren L. (1978) Straight with the Medicine. Washoe Followers of the Ti Pi Way Heyday Books, Berkeley, CA

Dowes, James F, (1966) The Two Worlds of the Washoe, New York Holt, Reinhart and Winston,

Gernes, Phyllis, Hidden in the Chaparral, (1979)

Nevers, John (1976) Wa She Su A Washoe Tribal History International Council of Nevada, University of Utah Printing Service Salt Lake City Utah

Siskin, Edgar E, (1983) Washoe Shamans University of Utah Press, Salt Lake City Utah

Sturtevant, William C, (1978) Handbook of North American Indians, Volume 8 and 11 Robert F, Heizer Smithsonian Institute Washington DC The Indians of California, (1994) Time Life Editors of Time Life Books Alexandria Virginia.

Oral Sources

Adams, Rick Nisenan Shaman
Bergen, Frank Ely Nevada Historian
January, Betty Clarksville Historian
Poor, Bill Store owner in Louisville
Paiute Members of the Nixon Indian Reservation
Peabody, George El Dorado Historian and outstanding American Citizen.
Schuster, Myrtle, Miwok friend of my mother from El Dorado California
Wheeldon, George Local Geologist

Numerous Washoe friends of My Grandfather who's names he could only vaguely remember.

I would also like to thank my Research Assistant, Editor and Friend Ben Atojino-Carrillo

The Washoe today

The Washoe have an incredible history and they are still here. They are some of the most friendly, hardest working people I know. If you are interested in contacting the Washoe Tribe here is some information you can use.

Washoe Tribal Headquarters
919 US Hwy 395 South
Gardenerville, NV 89410
1-800-76-WASHOE

Other books by Guy Nixon (Redcorn)

A RIVER DIVIDED
THE STORY & BIOGRAPHY OF
'CHIEF' COPPA HEMBO
1812-1898
The Success and Triumph of the Maidu and Washoe people under Coppa Hembo's leadership in El Dorado County California
By Jill (Redcorn) Kearney and Guy Nixon (Redcorn)

SLAVERY
IN THE
WEST
The untold story of the slavery of Native Americans in the West
By Guy Nixon
Red Corn

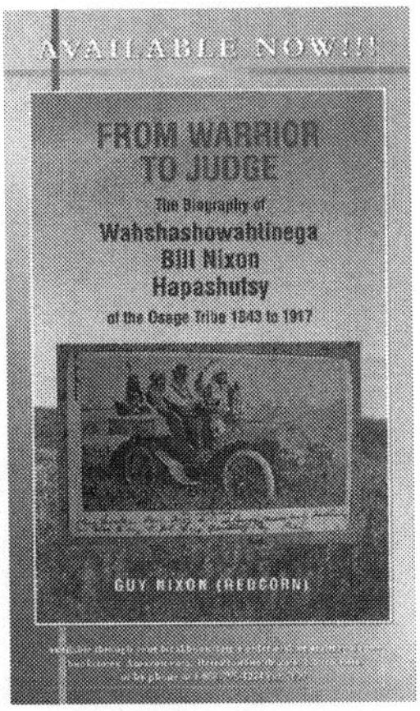
AVAILABLE NOW!!!
FROM WARRIOR
TO JUDGE
The Biography of
Wahshashowahtinega
Bill Nixon
Hapashutsy
of the Osage Tribe 1843 to 1917
GUY NIXON (REDCORN)

FINDING YOUR NATIVE
AMERICAN
ANCESTORS
By Guy Nixon
(Red Corn)

CALIFORNIA
WILDLIFE
ENCOUNTERS
Ben Nuckolls
and Guy Nixon

The Wild History of
Hell Hole and the Rubicon Country
1848 to 1948
El Dorado and Placer Counties California

In addition two titles are available only from the author

Sawmilling and Wood cut-ting for Little Operators

Heirloom Stories including the Story of Skipper the Stock Killer of Spanish Flat.

$15 each

5720 Spanish Flat Road

Garden Valley CA 95633

60965486R00058

Made in the USA
San Bernardino, CA
13 December 2017